# THE FINANCIAL ADVISOR'S GUIDE TO DIVORCE SETTLEMENT

## Helping Your Clients Make Sound Financial Decisions

**CAROL ANN WILSON**

*Foreword by Lynne Z. Gold-Bikin, J.D.*

**The Irwin/IAFP Series in Financial Planning**

IAFP

INTERNATIONAL ASSOCIATION
FOR FINANCIAL PLANNING

**IRWIN**

*Professional Publishing®*

Chicago • London • Singapore

This publication is designed to provide accurate and authoritative information in regard to the subject matter covered. It is sold with the understanding that neither the author or the publisher is engaged in rendering legal, accounting, or other professional service. If legal advice or other expert assistance is required, the services of a competent professional person should be sought.

*From a Declaration of Principles jointly adopted by a Committee of the American Bar Association and a Committee of Publishers.*

**◥▼ Times Mirror**
**M  Higher Education Group**

**Library of Congress Cataloging-in-Publication Data**
Wilson, Carol Ann.
    The financial advisor's guide to divorce settlement : helping your clients make sound financial decisions / Carol Ann Wilson : with foreword by Lynne Z. Gold-Bikin.
        p.  cm.
    Includes index.
    ISBN 0-7863-0851-6
    1. Divorced people--United States--Finance. Personal--Handbooks, manuals, etc.   2. Divorce settlements--United States--Handbooks, manuals, etc.   3. Marital property--Valuation--United States--Handbooks, manuals, etc.     I. Title.
HG179.W53516   1996
332.024 '0653—dc20                                                          96–12055

*Printed in the United States of America*
1 2 3 4 5 6 7 8 9 0 3 2 1 0 9 8 7 6

*To my husband of two years, Bill Fullmer,*
*who showed me that there is life after divorce.*

It is an unfortunate truth that divorce is a fact of life in the United States. As a matter of fact, the U.S. has a higher rate of divorce than any other industrial country. Since the dissolution of marriages is an everyday event, any way that the process can be made easier is of great interest to attorneys who practice in this area. As attorneys, we continue to search for products to make life easier for our clients, and we occasionally come upon a book that will shorten the divorce process. This particular book, *The Financial Advisor's Guide to Divorce Settlement,* is one of those products that eases the painful financial dissolution of a marriage.

Information is the most important resource in a fair and equitable settlement. Without information and a knowledge of the financial pot, the process cannot be fair. Consequently, finding a book such as *The Financial Advisor's Guide to Divorce Settlement* makes the discovery process that much easier.

A few years ago, I began using Divorce Plan™ software created by Carol Ann Wilson and Quantum Financial Inc. This software enables lawyers to project different financial scenarios, as well as predict the impact of the settlement decision years down the road. This particular software was and still is the best product of its kind to help professionals enable their clients to reach more equitable settlements. Now Wilson has taken the next step. Building upon the strengths of the software, she has written a book to enhance its use.

The process of divorce is more than simply dividing assets. Planning for the future is also an intricate part of the process. Just like the words "And they lived happily ever after" is not always the end of the story in a marriage, the divorce decree is not the end of the process for litigants. Planning for the future and understanding the impact of a settlement is equally important. *The Financial Advisor's Guide to Divorce Settlement* explains the process and the impact on the future of each litigant. The financial planner can utilize this book to help his or her client through the maze of financial decisions. More importantly, the book discusses and illustrates the ramifications of each of these decisions on the client's future.

Interestingly enough, in addition to a sound financial analysis, Ms. Wilson offers a groundbreaking suggestion: professionals should work together to help clients through the divorce process. This notion of teamwork among attorneys, financial planners, and mediators may seem unique, but with the changing attitudes toward litigation through the courts, it appears to be on the cutting edge of the changes in the divorce arena.

Having spent a number of years trying to develop programs to cut down on the divorce rate, I continue to realize that divorce will be with us for a long time. There is no way to make everyone happy. Given that fact, easing the process for those people going through it ought to be part of our arsenal. Additionally, anything that will help professionals work together to ease the divorce process is to be greatly admired. This book gives a road map to financial solutions, and a way for professionals to work together in the best interest of the client. Hopefully, it also aids the professional as constructively as possible in easing a couple's transition from being married to being single again. *The Financial Advisor's Guide to Divorce Settlement* provides the framework for this to happen. Utilization of the *Guide* in conjunction with the divorce plan software is greatly recommended.

**Lynne Z. Gold-Bikin, Esquire**
**Immediate Past Chair of the American**
**Bar Association Family Law Section, and**
**Fellow of the American and International**
**Academy of Matrimonial Lawyers**

"Divorce is often the biggest psychological crisis of an individual's life: that is, unless a child or spouse has died. On the stress 'Richter scale' divorce is in the top three," says Dr. Judith Briles, author of *Dollars and Sense of Divorce* and *Money Sense.*

In the late 1980s, I was hired by a woman from Connecticut who was getting divorced. She wanted me to represent her in court. As an expert witness, with my charts and graphs, I would be able to show why she should get the property and maintenance award she was requesting. I flew to Connecticut armed with my reports.

When we walked into the courtroom, the husband's attorney said to the judge, "Your Honor, we request a continuance so that we can find our own expert witness to rebut Ms. Wilson's testimony."

My client's attorney's response was, "Your Honor, there are no other experts like Ms. Wilson. She is the only one in the United States."

I thought to myself, Wow! Why should this judge listen to me if I'm the only one out there? So, right then, I decided to start teaching other financial planners how to develop the same expertise I have.

The notion of using my financial planning training to aid in equitable divorce settlements first came to me back in 1985. As a financial planner, I met with several women after their divorces were final. They seemed to be in severe financial trouble. I couldn't understand why, if the assets had been divided evenly, they should be having such financial problems. From these encounters, I developed the Divorce Plan™ software, which clearly showed me that *equal is not always equitable.*

I started gathering facts, reading books, attending legal education classes, talking to attorneys, and speaking to hundreds of people who had been through divorce. It became evident to me that something was wrong with the system that couples go through when they get divorced.

I believed there was the possibility of an equitable settlement that would help *preserve financial security after divorce.* That became my theme song. After several years of specializing in this niche, I heard it said that my work in this area had changed family law in Colorado. Attorneys were crafting more equitable settlements, and judges were handing down different rulings.

Well! If *I* could do it in Colorado, then others could do it in other states and *we* could make a difference. That was an exciting thought.

After the experience in Connecticut, I felt that if other financial planners all over the nation were doing the same thing—presenting data that showed the financial results of any given settlement—it would become an accepted, credible profession. It would become easier for all financial planners' expertise to be accepted in court. We would present data that would help people reach reasonable settlements. In turn, judges could—and would—make clearer decisions.

After handling 500 to 600 divorce cases and appearing over 100 times as an expert witness in court, and after speaking and teaching for several years, I saw the need to put all this information in one place. You are holding it—*The Financial Advisor's Guide to Divorce Settlement*. My only regret is that it wasn't in my hands when I started down the road in 1983 as a financial planner. I know it will be useful to you.

**Carol Ann Wilson**
**2724 Winding Trail Place**
**Boulder, CO 80304**
**303-447-1787**
**800-875-1760**
**e-mail: QuanFin.aol.com**
**http://www.webwise.com/divorce**

# ACKNOWLEDGMENTS

To Amy Ost, my publishing editor, who knew better than I did that I had this book in me.

To Judith Briles, a friend and mentor, to whom I am so indebted that I can never repay all the help she has given me.

To Kara Stewart, my copy editor, who made my work look good.

To Alan Gappinger, who has always been there to answer questions and give clarifications.

To Barbara Stark, Helen Stone, Ed Schilling, Ann Mygatt, Christine Coates, Michael Caplan, and Gail Heinzman for their contributions.

And to my husband, Bill Fullmer, whose understanding and support has been instrumental in writing this book.

# TABLE OF CONTENTS

## CHAPTER 1

# The New Divorce Niche

**M**ost people enter marriage believing in the words "till death do us part." They know their marriage will last forever; it will be one of the successful unions. They will beat the divorce odds. And they do, for a while. Then something happens and they realize that they may become one of the divorce statistics.

Divorce isn't something that happens to "other people" anymore. In fact, there are about 1.4 million divorces every year in the United States. That's at least 2.8 million husbands and wives who must face the challenges a breakup can cause—not counting their children, in-laws, relatives, and friends.

Consider these statistics:

Fifty percent of first marriages end in divorce.

Sixty percent of second marriages end in divorce.

In the first year after a divorce, the wife's standard of living often drops by 35 percent, while the husband's often increases.

Given the fact that divorce can and does happen, the solution is often not to prevent divorce but to help the process and the settlement be as equitable and as painless as possible. This has created a real market niche for professionals who are needed in all phases of the divorce process.

## THE WIFE'S POINT OF VIEW

The higher the income of the family, the wider the financial gap between divorced partners. The reason? Even though society is changing, most older couples still invest in the husband's career while the wife's job takes second place. And if the marriage lasts a long time, the wife has lost at least a decade of career growth. Although recent changes have started to alter this pattern, most older divorcing couples began their marriages in this traditional format. Divorcing men and women simply do not have equal income-producing potential. Instead, women who have spent 20 or 30 years in traditional marriages find themselves out in the cold with minimal marketable skills and minimal real job prospects.

The courts often ignore this crucial issue when dividing marital property. Most lawyers and judges try to provide equitable divorce settlements for both parties. However, without a comprehensive financial analysis, many wives end up in dire financial straits despite legislation designed to provide fair divorce settlements. A number of factors can contribute to an imbalance in a divorce settlement; however, one fundamental fact prevails: *traditional married couple's lifestyle is usually based on the husband's income.*

In dividing marital property, courts traditionally have overlooked one major asset of a marriage: the husband's career and the assets associated with it. These include his

- salary
- pension or retirement plan
- stock options
- health insurance
- life insurance
- disability insurance
- vacation pay
- sick pay
- education and training
- seniority and networking
- potential earning power

Unfortunately, many courts don't recognize career assets as property. In creating an equitable financial settlement, it is important to remember that *property is divided just once, but career assets continue to produce income regularly for years.*

The courts assume equal independence from both partners. Sometimes the court will award rehabilitative maintenance to ease a spouse into the work force. But the courts base these settlements on the assumption—often false—that both spouses can be equally self-sufficient. In reality, *marriage creates economic inequality.*

Research on divorce found that the most important issue for women is *survival.* They are terrified of becoming bag ladies! Yet this fear isn't as irrational as it may sound. In the late 1980s, several states set up task forces to study gender bias in the courts. For example, in Colorado, one section of the task force was charged with the area of divorce. It studied cases taken directly from the court files. The parameters were that (1) the marriage have lasted 12 years or longer, (2) the case be decided by a judge as opposed to being settled out of court (the task force wanted to see the results of what the judges were doing), and (3) there was a minimum of $10,000 in positive net worth.[1]

Out of 28 cases, the average length of marriage was 20.5 years. At the time of divorce, the average age of the wife was 44, the husband, 45. Eleven of the 28 families had net assets of less than $50,000 at the time of divorce, 10 had net assets of $100,000 or more.[2]

Figure 1–1 graphs the results of this study. It is a composite of the 28 cases, showing the average net worth of husband and wife at the time of the divorce (based on the court-ordered property division) and the projected change in net worth for each of them. At the time of the court order, the wife's average net worth is slightly greater than the husband's because she is usually allocated less of the marital debt. Within four years of the divorce, however, the wife's projected net worth declines by 25 percent while the husband's nearly doubles. Within eight years of the divorce, the wife will have a negative net worth while the husband's projected net worth is approximately $200,000.[3]

In gathering data, besides looking at the court files, the Colorado task force interviewed many divorced men and women. One women told her story about the maintenance award after 38 years of marriage during which she was not employed. The judge ordered her husband to pay her $300 per month for two years. He awarded the house, appraised at $160,000, to the wife, and all the other assets, including a retirement

---

1. Colorado Supreme Court Task Force on Gender Bias in the Courts, 1990, p. 7.
2. Ibid. p. 14.
3. Ibid. p. 14.

# FIGURE 1-1

## Net Worth

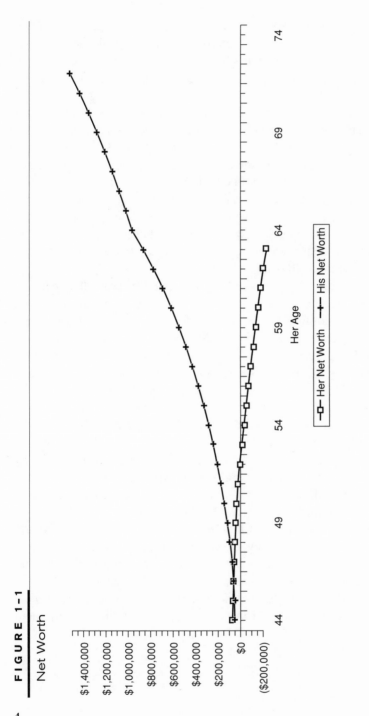

Her Age

—□— Her Net Worth   —+— His Net Worth

fund, to the husband, saying, "Mother has been out of the work force, and if we gave her all that money she wouldn't know how to handle it."[4]

Another woman told the Colorado task force that she had been awarded a tractor as part of the property settlement but her exhusband refused to deliver it. She had tried for four years to get the original order enforced, without success. One district judge gave her former husband permission to continue using the tractor. When her lawyer objected, the judge asked her what she was going to do with the tractor.[5]

## THE HUSBAND'S POINT OF VIEW

The awakening of the men's movement in this country is providing insight into the pain that men experience. The divorce process is a common source of much of that pain. Surprisingly, in many cases it is the man—not the women—who is paralyzed by emotions. Feeling terribly victimized, men sometimes conclude that courts agree with the cynical saying, "What's his is theirs and what's hers is hers."

*Men have several very real concerns.* The number one concern for fathers with young children often is how the divorce will affect their relationship with their children. Even though we hear about fathers who abandon their children after divorce, this is not the prevailing behavior. During divorce, men fight for the right to participate in the lives of their children. Only if denied that right do they sometimes walk away in frustration and discontinue child support payments.

**The Washington State Task Force on Gender and Justice in the Courts found that only 10 percent of all wives being divorced were awarded maintenance and the average amount was $432 per month for an average length of 2.6 years. The national average as of spring 1986 had 15 percent of wives receiving an average of $329 per month.[6]**

---

4. Ibid. p. 20.
5. Ibid. p. 21.
6. Washington State Task Force on Gender and Justice in the Courts, 1989.

Fathers dread their lack of control in the divorce situation and fear the court's power to decree the most intimate details of their relationship with children. The fact that a man and woman no longer get along with each other does not mean that a father loves his children less. In fact, in many cases going through a divorce takes the father through an educational process that brings him closer to his own hidden emotions, paving the way toward a warmer, more participative role as a dad.

After the issue of children, a man's second concern is often the prospect of paying lifetime alimony to his exwife. No one wants to be tied into that possibility. Men want an end to the payments. They believe they cannot get on with their own lives as long as they have to pay out a large portion of their income to someone who is no longer a part of their lives. They see this as keeping the relationship going with no possibility of relief. They really do not understand why, when a relationship is at an end, they should have to support this person indefinitely. Moreover, they cannot understand why a woman would want this continued enmeshment, either.

Having to pay out large sums in the first few years after a divorce for things like child support, alimony, and attorneys' fees (both his and hers), as well as property settlement, means that a man's discretionary income may suffer greatly. He frequently feels that he has been taken to the cleaners and that he is doomed to pay for the divorce forever. In some cases, he may be right. But statistics show that in the vast majority of cases, the financial effects of divorce are relatively short-lived. Men can take solace in the fact that their earning potential is almost always higher than the exwife's and they will eventually be financially better off than the exwife.

A third critical concern to men is sharing their pensions. A man feels he earned the pension and he should not have to share it with anyone. It's interesting that, in many cases, the man will agree to a 50/50 property split and give the wife other assets in exchange for keeping his pension—"just don't touch my pension!" It becomes an extremely emotional issue that can steer a man in the wrong direction!

A fourth concern for the self-employed man is his business. If it has significant value, this can be an area of great concern for both sides. All too often it is the only marital asset of real value and, since it cannot be divided, paying the wife her half of the value can be a real problem.

Sometimes this is solved with a property settlement note. (Chapter 4 gives more information on this.) However, some judges have difficulty with this arrangement.

A universal concern is a perception that the deck is stacked against men from the beginning because of pressures from highly visible feminists and a sympathetic press. Men feel that they are made to pay the price for a minority of husbands and fathers who ignore their responsibilities. It is the experience of many men that they are assumed guilty for the breakup of the marriage and that they must pay in order to atone for this sin.

The Colorado task force received a few complaints from men who felt they had been victims of gender bias in awards of spousal maintenance or child support. For example, one man stated, "The purpose of maintenance is to sustain the weaker of the parties, when that one has contributed to the rise of the union by sacrifice of career or education, until such time that the weaker one becomes established and self-sufficient. In my case the wife was the direct cause of the financial problems of the union and should not be rewarded for that. This lady has no intention to re-train, or have a career."[7]

## IS AN EQUITABLE DIVORCE SETTLEMENT POSSIBLE?

Divorce often has a devastating impact on everyone involved. While some couples effect a civilized divorce and remain semifriends, many couples go through World War III, which, especially if they end up in court, can permanently damage the rest of their lives.

Can something be done to lessen the negative impact of divorce? Are equitable settlements really possible? Yes.

However, few judges and attorneys are financial experts. Financial analysis of the outcome of possible settlements is complex and requires substantial experience. When legal expertise is not matched with sophisticated financial projections, an apparently equal division of property can leave the lower- or nonearning spouse destitute within a few years.

Contrary to popular belief, arranging a settlement that benefits the lower-earning spouse does not necessarily harm the higher-earning spouse. In addition, even though a lower standard of living may be anticipated, it does not have to be dramatically lower for either spouse.

---

7. Colorado Supreme Court Task Force on Gender Bias in the Courts, 1990.

Although it is impossible to predict the future, sophisticated software methodology can be used to forecast the eventual financial outcome of specific divorce settlements. Such software allows judges, lawyers, and divorcing couples to compare the outcome of various suggested settlements. The program can be used to test different scenarios, such as higher or longer-lasting maintenance, disproportionate property division, and reduced standards of living.

With available software, along with professionals versed in the intricacies of putting together equitable final settlements and experts dedicated to helping couples avoid the court battle, a more humane result can be accomplished. This book provides the tools to getting a broad-based understanding of how to do this.

## CHAPTER 2

# The Financial Advisor's Role

---

**THE AFTERMATH OF DIVORCE: A PARABLE**

After her divorce, Joyce went to a financial planner to see how to best reposition her assets. Together, they decided to do a total financial plan for her. During the planning session, it became apparent that during her marriage her husband had done all of the investing. He chose all of the investments, made all the decisions, and invested all the money.

At divorce time, he said, "Let's just split everything 50/50. You take this half of the investments and I will take that half. Is that OK?"

Joyce answered, "Well, I guess that sounds pretty fair. That's OK with me."

Unfortunately, there was something she did not know or understand. Neither did her attorney, and neither did the judge. They didn't realize that Joyce was getting half of the investments with *all* the tax recapture. Her 50/50 split cost her an additional $18,000 in taxes. If Joyce had seen a financial planner *before* the divorce was final, she would have been in a better position to formulate a more equitable settlement.

---

This parable has an unfortunate ending, but predivorce financial counseling can help people arrive at a fair settlement for all involved.

Who do people turn to for such assistance? When people think about getting divorced, the first professional that comes to mind is an attorney. Typically, a financial advisor—whether it be their CPA, their financial planner, or a Certified Divorce Planner—isn't thought about until later. Unfortunately, too much later.

Financial woes can tear a marriage apart and are often the primary problem that eventually leads to divorce. If couples can't solve their financial problems during the marriage, why do they think they will be able to agree on the financial issues of divorce? They have questions like

How do we value our property?

Who gets what property?

What are the tax issues?

How do we divide retirement funds and future pensions?

How will the lower-earning spouse survive?

What kind of additional help or support does that person need?

Who gets the house?

Will that person have to pay capital gains tax?

Who gets the children?

Who will pay for college, for summer camp, for orthodontia for the children?

What happens if a paying exspouse dies?

Many attorneys also struggle with the intricate financial details that concern tax issues, IRS rulings, capital gains, dividing pensions, and the like. The attorneys attended law school to become expert in the law, not to become financial experts. Fortunately, however, many attorneys are aware of their shortcomings in financial expertise and are willing to get help from a financial expert. That's where you, the financial planner, come in. Some attorneys try to do it all themselves and many of them have made serious blunders.

## WHAT IS THE FINANCIAL PLANNER'S ROLE?

There are many titles for a financial expert: Certified Public Accountant (CPA), financial planner, Certified Financial Planner (CFP), Chartered Financial Consultant (ChFC), economist, accountant, and Certified Divorce Planner (CDP).

A Certified Divorce Planner is a new type of professional. This person is often a Certified Financial Planner who has taken additional intensive training to become skilled in working with people during divorce, becoming part of the divorce team with the attorney, dealing with all the financial issues in each case, and appearing as an expert witness if needed. This designation and training is given by the Quantum Institute for Professional Divorce Planning.[1]

The role of a financial planner, as opposed to a generic financial expert, is to help people achieve their financial goals regardless of whether they are divorcing or happily married. After deciding what the goals are, the next step is to look at what needs to be done to achieve those goals. These goals can be from one year to 50 years in the future. Looking that far into the future requires certain assumptions about income, expenses, inflation, interest rates, return on investments, and retirement needs. After the assumptions are made and plugged in, the scenario needs to be reviewed on a regular basis to see if they are still on track.

In other words, the financial planner looks at financial results in the future based on certain assumptions made today. Conversely, the CPA typically looks at the details of the scenario as it is today and makes no future projections. These ideologies can certainly be blended for the best interest of the client.

Everyone in the midst of divorce is understandably concerned about their financial future and how the decisions they make today are going to affect their future. It behooves them to make some educated guesses as to what the future will hold based on what their final decisions are today.

A financial planner is well versed in interviewing clients to find out what their future goals are, when they want to retire, how much risk they are willing to take with their investments, what kind of a living style they want, what kind of education they want for their children, and so on.

Certified Financial Planners, on the other hand, are also trained in tax issues, estate planning, retirement planning, investment planning, insurance planning, cash flows, and budgeting. What better professional to have involved to help spouses reach a reasonable settlement that will come closest to reaching both their goals.

---

1. Quantum Institute for Professional Divorce Planning in Boulder, Colorado, offers a two-day intensive training for professionals and certifies them as Certified Divorce Planners. The agenda includes an overview of the divorce market, tax laws of divorce, division of property, alimony, child support, and pensions as well as being an expert witness in court and marketing these services. Also included is hands-on training with the Divorce Plan™ software. Phone 1-800-875-1760.

Few win in a divorce. It seems that no matter how much money there is, each spouse has to adjust the standard of living after the divorce to make things work out. But there are solutions that can minimize the potentially devastating effects. It is safe to assume that both of the divorcing spouses loved each other once upon a time. Hopefully, at divorce time, they have some concern about how the other will fare after the divorce.

## IF THE CLIENT IS THE WIFE

In a traditional marriage where the husband has worked and the wife has stayed home to care for the children, the wife client poses concerns about having enough income to live on to continue her previous standard of living. Sometimes, this is just impossible. Many couples can't afford their standard of living with one household, let alone two, and they end up with large credit card debt. Asking an ex-husband to pay enough to allow his ex-wife to continue her previous lifestyle may not be realistic. After looking at the numbers, the expert should counsel the wife about expectations. Perhaps a lesson in budgeting is appropriate.

It's also important to acknowledge the high degree of emotional stress during this time. Both parties hurt. There's often anger. Territories and turfs are drawn. The financial planner can be a key facilitator in moving either or both parties toward some type of therapy or professional counseling.

Another concern for the wife is whether to go back to work or whether to train for a better job. Typically, in the traditional marriage, either the wife is not working outside the home or else she has a very low-paying job. A career counselor may be useful in testing the wife for skills and possibilities in the job market.

The wife often gets custody of the children. This has several effects that often are not considered. First, as the children get older, they really do cost more to maintain! They have more expensive hobbies: skiing, biking, musical instruments, computers, and so on. They eat more. Their clothes are more expensive. They might need orthodontia. Items needed for school cost much more than a few pencils and paper. As schools cut back, parents are required to supply *all* the essentials.

Second, having custody of the children will influence what kind of job the wife gets. It will be very difficult to develop a career where, to get ahead and earn the top salary, she will have to work nights or weekends or spend time traveling. So her primary career will likely have to be flexible to allow her to care for the children.

A third effect of having custody of the children is the emotional and psychological difficulty of dealing with children's issues and problems on a daily basis without a second parent to share in this. All parents can relate to this.

Many wives have not been involved with the financial issues during the marriage and just don't know what it will take to live comfortably. They don't know what all the assets are and which ones they should ask for. They don't know if they should take one of the rental properties and become a landlord. They don't know the effect of getting future benefits from the pension versus taking a cash payout today. A lot of educating has to be done in some of these cases. Many attorneys bring in a financial expert to take part in this educating process.

## IF THE CLIENT IS THE HUSBAND

The husband may be very astute concerning the financial issues. He may offer to split the property evenly and give the wife some alimony so that she can get educated enough to get a good job. Sometimes, when a husband and wife no longer want to be married to each other, the husband's opinion of the wife's job or potential job skills may escalate to a high degree.

The husband is concerned about losing his children. Divorcing his wife often results in divorcing his children too. The ex-wife may find it impossible to speak kindly of the ex-husband and this can affect the way the children react toward him. The ex-spouses may even move apart geographically, which makes it more difficult to have a continuing sharing relationship with the children. Some attorneys urge their male clients to ask for custody of the children, whether they want them or not, to use as a bargaining tool in settling other matters such as division of property and maintenance.

Some husbands are terrified of losing their net worth. The thought of giving away half of what they have built up over the years is not acceptable to them. Other husbands, out of guilt, offer most of the assets to the ex-wife.

If the husband has been the higher-earning spouse, he typically will not ask for help from a financial consultant. He may feel that he understands the financial picture more than his wife does and he might not understand why she hires outside experts when he has shown her a very fair way of dividing their assets. If, however, the wife is asking for more than he feels he can afford to pay, he will want reports to show that he is unable to meet her demands.

## WHAT ELSE WILL THE FINANCIAL ADVISOR DO?

Many divorces involve a pension that needs to be evaluated. Financial experts are trained in figuring the present value of a pension.

Most divorcing couples own a house. A financial expert can calculate the answers to questions about the basis, the capital gains, whether it is feasible to keep the house, and who needs to buy what after the divorce is final.

When investments are involved, the financial expert can evaluate them as to their basis, the tax issues if they are sold, how risky they are to keep, what kind of return they are producing, and so on.

A financial expert will look at inflation's long-term effect on how much is needed at retirement, how much needs to be saved, how much can be spent compared to how much is earned, and so on. This can lead to good planning for the future and may be one of the most important parts of advising during the divorce process.

If a settlement cannot be reached on all of the issues, the case will probably end up in court with a judge making the final decisions. A financial expert can appear as an expert witness who shows, with reports and graphs, the result that any given settlement will have on each spouse. This information is helpful to the judge in coming to the final conclusions.

The financial expert is thus a very important part of the divorce process and should be brought in on most cases to be part of the team. There have been real liability issues in the past where financial issues were not looked at carefully enough up front by the attorney.

## CHAPTER 3

# From the Attorney's Point of View

**N**ot all attorneys are going to hire financial planners to help them present and analyze the financial data in a divorce case. Many attorneys believe they know it all—otherwise we wouldn't have so many lawyer jokes! And then there are the attorneys who like to keep things stirred up because they earn more money that way. These are not the kinds of attorneys who hire the outside financial experts.

Instead, the attorneys who hire financial experts are the ones who want to help their clients get the most favorable results possible. In general, they are the more caring attorneys. And, yes, they do exist no matter how many jokes you hear.

Don't worry that you'll never be hired by the attorney who likes to keep things stirred up. That is fine. In fact, you do not want to work with that kind of person. They just want to enhance the adversarial relationship between the two spouses. The more they fight, the higher the attorney bills. You want to work with an attorney whose objective is to help the client settle the case. Fortunately, there are plenty of such attorneys out there.

In this section, you will hear the opinions of two divorce lawyers—Barbara Stark and Ann Mygatt—straight from the horse's mouth, so to speak.

## BARBARA STARK

The following is from Barbara Stark, J.D., a fellow of the American Academy of Matrimonial Lawyers. She is a nationally recognized speaker and frequently lectures to professional and lay audiences.

*     *     *     *

The average rate of collection for a divorce lawyer is about 70 percent. This means that they only earn money on 70 percent of the hours they work. Understandably, there is a great deal of price pressure on their hourly fee because of all of their uncollectable bills.

However, as attorney fees go up, the client is more and more unwilling to pay these fees. This resistance is due not only to economic reasons, but also to clients' unwillingness to engage in the battle that these high fees represent. They do not want to go to court in the first place and they certainly don't want to use all their kid's college money on lawyers arguing.

It boils down to this: Two people who were perhaps unable to handle their joint finances when they were married are now divorcing and there simply is not enough money for their current needs, much less financing some really expensive matrimonial lawyer.

Also, ferocious competition puts pressure on divorce lawyers' fees. Every lawyer has the pressures of liability insurance, increasing overhead, and shrinking market share. To meet these financial burdens, even lawyers who specialize in other forms of law will start to accept divorce cases. Economically, they cannot afford to refer those cases out anymore.

The team of the lawyer and the financial planner involves a blending of expertise. An experienced lawyer is someone who can teach you. As a financial planner, you need to come into this business knowing the divorce laws, knowing the case trends, and knowing what is going on in the courts. But as that knowledge grows, a good lawyer is going to teach you as you go through cases because you and the lawyer are going to be sharing ideas. Actually, you will develop with a good divorce lawyer a sense of mutual respect and a rhythm to a relationship in which you work together really well. That is the ideal in terms of working with lawyers.

But there are a lot of inexperienced lawyers out there. The reason? There are simply too many lawyers. Nearly every lawyer who hangs out his or her shingle is taking divorce cases but does not necessarily have a high level of expertise. It probably will not surprise you that when attorneys come right out of law school, they have no idea how to try a divorce case. They do not learn how to do this in law school.

Just because you are working with a lawyer, do not assume the lawyer knows what he or she is doing. If you are an inexperienced financial planner working with an inexperienced lawyer, you both are going to be working your way through the case together, which may be a bit awkward because the lawyer may rely excessively on you. The lawyer could be perceiving you as the expert while you are perceiving the lawyer as the expert. You have to keep the communication very open so that you have a feeling of where you are going as a team.

Here's the final point to remember. If you want to build a good reputation in your community—both in court and out of court—the most important things you have are your credibility and your integrity. You never want to lose them. There are lawyers (and financial planners, for that matter) in your community who do not have credibility and do not have integrity. Be cautious and check out the lawyers for whom you work. There will always be another case, but you only have one reputation. You want to protect that reputation as carefully as you can. Make sure that working with that lawyer passes the "smell test" with you. If it does not smell right, if it does not feel right, get out of the situation because it is not worth it to you in the long run.

## ANN MYGATT

Ann Mygatt, J.D., (former prosecutor for the district attorney's office in Boulder, Colorado), has been practicing family law since 1983. She had the following to say about working with lawyers.

*       *       *       *

You, the financial planner, are extremely important in this business because we lawyers want to settle our cases. We really do not want to go to trial but sometimes it's unavoidable. If we have to go to trial, we need you as an expert witness.

As a financial planner hoping to work with lawyers, there are three things you need to know: how to work with lawyers, the legal pitfalls, and finally how to market yourself to divorce attorneys.

# How to Work with Lawyers

How do financial planners fit into the picture of a divorce trial? More than anything else, you have to be flexible. You have to play many different roles when you work with a divorce attorney. Not only are you on the team, you are a critical member of that team. At any time during the divorce process, you may play any one or all of the following roles depending when you get the case initially: strategist, mediator, negotiator, client expectations manager, evidence presenter, and advisor/trial preparation assistant.

***1. Strategist***   Before the case is even filed, I like to use the financial planner as a strategist. We need to know what the financial implications of different divorce settlements are going to be.

For instance, in a case that I worked on a couple of years ago, a woman was getting divorced after a 25-year marriage. The offspring, two daughters, were just about out of college. The woman had expectations that when she became divorced from her husband—who was earning about $95,000 a year—she would essentially be taken care of for the rest of her life.

She needed to know from a financial planner what was going to happen. Even though her husband had earned a significant salary, she did not have a realistic view of what she could expect at the divorce. They did not have very much property, and they had spent almost everything they had earned during the marriage. In addition, she hadn't worked much outside the home. It was very important for her to spend time with a financial planner to go over the charts that explained what she might realistically receive.

***2. Mediator***   One often overlooked use for a financial planner is in the role of mediator. I have a financial planner meet with my client a couple of times and then with both the husband and the wife together. Then we all go through the charts and the explanations of what there is in the way of assets and income, and what the future will look like. Sometimes out of that process, either with or without attorneys, the couple can come up with a mediated settlement that they both accept. If so, they won't need to have a trial in court.

***3. Negotiator***   The role of negotiator brings to mind an amusing case. Two people had been married for about 15 or 20 years and they had spent some time in Southeast Asia. Each had an import–export business and, not surprisingly, the two greatest assets of their marriage were their businesses. They made a fair amount of money from those businesses but they were not willing to agree as to what the values were. Each said, "Your business is worth more than my business, and I want to be compensated for that." To get them to finally agree to a value, we had each person pick his or her own expert. Then we put the experts together and said, "You come up with a number that would be fair for each of these businesses." Lo and behold, they did and the clients had to agree to that valuation.

### *4. Client Expectations Manager*   I think this is probably one of the most important roles that a financial planner can take in this process, and it is something that the lawyer can't do. When I have a client in my office—it doesn't matter whether it is a husband or a wife—I know the person sometimes needs a reality check. I will send him or her to a financial planner and say, "Sit down and talk." These people need to know the truth. Many people come into my office with either grandiose expectations of what they can do or grandiose expectations of entitlement, and they need to be given a dose of reality. Sometimes it is easier for me to use a financial planner to do that than to do it myself.

### *5. Evidence Presenter*   Being an evidence presenter in a case is critical. The lawyer has assembled a number of different experts for different issues in a case, and you may be there for one part of that case. In this role you are, more than anything else, there to translate for people who don't understand financial matters, including the lawyers.

In fact, in the middle of one trial, I was cross-examining their witness. All of a sudden, I thought, Everybody is talking gibberish—I do not understand what anybody said in the last 10 minutes. So I asked for a break, I took my expert out in the hallway, and said, "Tell me what just happened. What did he just say?" The expert calmed me down and brought me back to reality. It helped a lot because the expert's skills as a translator were good.

As attorneys, numbers and financial data are not our area of expertise, so we really depend on you, the financial planner, to translate what you know into information that makes sense. Translation was what I needed, and after about 10 minutes in the hallway, I understood. I brushed myself off, went back into the court room, and finished up the case.

Basically, the financial expert carried that case, and we got a great result. The reason we did is because we had someone in court who could present (1) the evidence of the wife's reasonable needs and (2) the fact that the husband had the ability to pay her maintenance and still meet his own reasonable needs. It also helped that we could show the judge exactly what the financial circumstances were now and what they would be 5, 10, and 15 years from now.

**6. Advisor/Trial Preparation Assistant**   More than anything else, a lawyer needs you to help us optimize our results to the client. You can make us look good to both the client and the judge.

## The Dangers and Pitfalls of Working with Divorce Lawyers

### Personality Style
The first thing to remember about working with divorce lawyers is that we are a certain type. When you get a lot of divorce lawyers together, you are going to get a group of people that are not just lawyers, but a unique brand of lawyers. We tend to have the lawyer qualities of being compulsive and competitive. We are also intelligent, interesting people. We have wide interests. You can scratch a lawyer and, beneath the lawyer surface, sometimes find a poet.

Divorce lawyers are people who like action. They are not the kind of people you would find working on an IBM case that lasts 10 or 15 years. These are people with short attention spans. A case comes into my office and a year later it is finished.

When one of my cases is over, the first thing I do is file a motion to withdraw, because I am on to the next case. That is part of who I am. I like the action. I like the variety, the movement. I like people in transition—people who are changing and in transformation. I like being a part of that transformation. I like the drama and I think divorce lawyers tend—as a group—to be emotional, flamboyant, and dramatic. They handle high stress all the time.

### Adversary System
It is a fact that our courts are set up to be an adversarial system. When you are set for trial, you are at war. This means people who are involved

as litigants and participants in this process are afraid. When you are dealing with people who are afraid, you are in very dangerous territory. People who are afraid become likely to lash out, they may be irrational, and they may be looking for someone to blame if they do not get what they want.

These are things to keep in mind when you are working with divorce attorneys, because divorce lawyers have the highest incidence of grievances and the highest incidence of malpractice claims of any area of law.

You are going to be working in that arena. You cannot assume anything. You cannot assume that the judge knows anything unless it is put in evidence as a fact, and only then might the court find that there is enough evidence to find in favor of your client.

## Pressures within the Legal Profession

One of the greatest concerns of the American Bar Association as well as the state bar associations is that professionalism has declined so much in the past few years. Reasons for that include there are too many lawyers, there are not enough jobs, there is too much competition, and there are no mentors.

As a result, a kind of a subculture of Rambo tactics and real viciousness has developed. It seems to come out more often with divorce and personal injury attorneys than any other kind. In fact, I have heard it said that divorce attorneys are really the Rodney Dangerfields of the legal profession.

## Technological Information Revolution

In the past few years, attorneys have significantly changed how they run their law offices. They now have access to PCs so they can run software programs. However, most lawyers in your market are going to be like me. As an attorney, I am your client in more ways than one. I am a sole practitioner. I do not have the resources of a large law firm. I need somebody to help me through the thicket of technological tools that I do not have the time or inclination to master. Though this technological information revolution confuses me, it probably is one of your greatest advantages in this business.

## Professional Burnout

Finally, as a group, lawyers tend to have good staying power, but most divorce attorneys burn out after about 10 years. Either that, or we learn how to pace our practices, which may mean taking off for a couple of years and doing something completely different.

# How to Market Yourself to a Divorce Attorney

To have the best chance for success, there a few things to keep in mind:

**1.** *Professional demeanor.* Do not show up in blue jeans or chew gum. Like it or not, first impressions count. Look professional and you will come across as the expert you are. This will build clients' confidence in you.

**2.** *Knowledge and competence.* Your knowledge and competence are what make people come back. Your expertise makes you necessary. You are the solution to our problem.

**3.** *Common sense.* Common sense involves knowing how much time, money, and effort to put into a case. You do not want to overmarket yourself. Not every case needs a financial planner, and you do not want to market yourself to everyone. The effort that goes into your marketing should be consistent with that realization.

**4.** *Flexibility.* You also need to be able to look at a situation when you are asked to do something and be able to jump into it where you can. You might have varying levels of flexibility so you need to know your limitations.

**5.** *Visibility and promotion.* You need to be visible—you need to show people how they need you. There are a lot of different ways of doing that: Network, write articles, put on small conventions or seminars for people. You can do this with an attorney, another financial planner, or another expert.

I was sitting in court one Friday morning. One of the lawyers had brought in a financial planner to testify. At the end of the hearing, about five of the lawyers in the audience asked for her card because she had done such a good job. She was up there promoting not only her client's case but herself and the field as well. You never know where you might meet new clients.

No matter what you are doing or where you are, always figure you might run into a client or potential clients.

**6.** *Know yourself.* The last thing to keep in mind is knowing yourself. You may not be the right financial planner for a particular client. The more you work in this field, the more you are going to know your limitations. You are going to know your strengths and your weaknesses, and how you can help people. Part of your strength as an expert is knowing when to say, "No, I cannot work on this case," and having the courage to decline a case.

When you've had more experience as an expert witness, you'll know how you can best work with that divorce lawyer in that particular case.

## CHAPTER 4

# Property Valuations and Settlement

**W**hen looking at the property issues in divorce, the couple always asks three questions: "What constitutes property, what is it worth, and how will it be divided?" In addition to those items traditionally seen as property, today's couples must take into consideration career assets.

Although each couple is different, there are some averages when it comes to property. "Most divorcing couples have household furnishings (89%), cars (71%), and some savings in the form of money in bank accounts, stocks, or bonds (61%). Almost half (46%) of the couples own or are buying a family home, which is likely to be a couple's most valuable asset. Only a small proportion of divorcing couples have a pension (24%), a business (11%), or other real estate (11%)."[1]

It has been said that most divorcing couples have a net worth of less than $20,000. If this is so, it may be that couples are investing in their careers and earning capabilities instead of their savings accounts. They may see their careers as being more valuable than tangible assets. Because future income is typically of greater value than property, the main financial issues in divorce, particularly for women and children, are those of spousal and child support.

---

1. Lenore Weitzman, *The Divorce Revolution,* Chapter 3 ("The Nature of Marital Property"). New York: The Free Press (a Division of Macmillan, Inc.), 1985.

## WHAT CONSTITUTES PROPERTY?

Property includes such assets as the family home, rental property, cars, and art or antique collections. It can also include bank accounts, mutual funds, stocks and bonds, life insurance cash value, IRAs, and retirement plans. As you can see, there is virtually no limit to what can be considered property.

However, although the laws vary from state to state, property is usually divided into just two categories: separate property and marital property. In general, separate property includes what a person brings into the marriage, inherits during the marriage, and receives as a gift during the marriage. On the other hand, marital property is everything acquired during the marriage no matter whose name it's in. In some (but not all) states, marital property also includes the increase in value of separate property.

What kind of state do you live in? That is, what rules of property division does your state follow? There are two different types of states—community property states and equitable distribution states—and the differences are subtle. Once you know how your state handles property division, you can help your client decide which property is the husband's, the wife's, and the couple's.

Community property states first identify the property that is not subject to division of the court, which is the husband's and wife's separate property. The court then may decide on how the couple's property is divided. The husband's or wife's *separate property* generally is owned before the marriage, or obtained by gift or inheritance. Everything else is *community property* and is subject to *equal* division.

Equitable distribution states, on the other hand, usually agree that the couple's property—*marital property*—is divided between the husband and wife *equitably*. (For more information, see the section "Equal versus Equitable" on page 30.) There are three types of equitable distribution states, based on how they identify marital property.

The first type of equitable distribution state identifies marital property as all property except property that the husband or wife brought into the marriage or obtained by gift or inheritance at any time. This definition is nearly identical to that held by community property states. It too upholds the view that, when in doubt, the property is marital. The major difference is only in the language.

The second type of equitable distribution state says that regardless of how property was brought to the marriage or who has title, all property of both spouses is subject to division and disposition at divorce. These states do not differentiate between marital and nonmarital (or separate) property. Such states divide property fairly and equitably, and may allow property brought into the marriage or received by gift or inheritance to go to the other spouse if this form of distribution would be more fair under the circumstances. However, the source of the property (gift, inheritance, owned prior to marriage, etc.) is often very important in this decision.

The final category of equitable distribution state is simply a mix of rules. Such states do use equity as a means of division, but don't exempt all gifts, inheritances, or property brought into marriage. Also, they do exempt one or two of these types of property.

As you've seen, these different types of state are not all that different. They all follow the general idea of dividing property to achieve fairness. The differences are (1) the starting point and (2) the rules each type of state uses to reach a fair result. For example, some start from the standpoint that all property is subject to division by the court, and then, depending on the circumstances, give property that was owned prior to the marriage or was acquired by gift or inheritance to the parties that owned it or received it. Other states start with the notion that such property isn't subject to distribution by the court at all, and thus narrow down the issues to be decided.

While there are several types of property states, your client can achieve much the same outcome in all of them depending on how the information is presented.

## WHAT IS PROPERTY WORTH?

The best way to explain property values and types is by examples of situations similar to those you'll encounter in your practice.

Let's say Beth and her husband are getting a divorce. Assume that when Beth got married, she had $1,000 in a savings account. During the marriage, her $1,000 earned $100 in interest and now the account is worth $1,100. She did not add her husband's name to the account. Her property is $1,000 because she kept it in her name only and, in some states, the $100 in interest goes into the pot of marital assets to be divided because that is the increase in value of her separate property. If Beth had put her husband's name on the account, she would have turned the entire account into a marital asset.

In second or third marriages, both people may bring houses into the marriage. Suppose that when she got married, Beth had a house that she kept in her name only. At that time, the house was worth $100,000 and had $70,000 mortgage on it, so the equity was $30,000. Now Beth is getting divorced. Today the house is worth $150,000. The mortgage is down to about $50,000. Equity has increased to $100,000.

| At Marriage | At Divorce |
|---|---|
| $100,000 value | $150,000 value |
| −70,000 mortgage | −50,000 mortgage |
| $ 30,000 equity | $100,000 equity |

Although these numbers would seem to lead to only one conclusion in the valuation of property, the following is likely to happen. Beth's attorney is going to say, "The increase in value is the difference between the $100,000 and $150,000—or $50,000—and that is what we will put into the marital pot of assets." Beth's husband's attorney is going to say, "Oh no, the increase in value is the increase in the equity, or $70,000." So who is right? Beth asks her attorney, "What does the law say?" The lawyer replies, "There is no law. We make the laws every time we go to court." In many states, the outcome of Beth's case depends on how the attorneys argue it and how the judge decides it.

Let's reverse the situation. Assume Beth put her husband's name on the deed to the house when they got married. After all, they were going to be together for the rest of their lives. As soon as she put her husband's name on the deed, she gave what is called a presumptive gift to the marriage. This turned the house into a marital asset.

Now let's assume that Beth's aunt died and left her $10,000. That is an inheritance. If she put it into an account with her name only on it, then at the divorce, it is her separate property except for the increase in value. It is the same with a gift. When she received the gift or inheritance, if she put it into a joint account, she turned that money into marital property.

Beth saves $100 of her paycheck every month. She puts this $100 a month into an account with her name only, and now it is worth $2,600. At her divorce, is this money separate or marital property? This is fairly straightforward. It is marital property because it is acquired during the marriage, no matter whose name it's in.

What if Beth owned stock worth $10,000 when she got married? If on the day of the divorce it is worth $9,000, is that a $1,000 marital loss? Yes. If there is a marital increase on one asset, it can be offset with a marital loss.

Assume that when Beth got married, her husband gave her an eight-carat diamond ring. Let's assume that they are in court and she is testifying that the ring was a gift from her husband so it is her personal property. He says, "Are you kidding? I would not *give* you an eight-carat diamond. That was an investment, so therefore it is marital property." The judge decides. However sexist it may seem, it has been my experience that women get to keep their jewelry, their furs, and similar types of gifts. Men get to keep their tools, their guns, and their golf clubs.

Let's say Beth's husband had given her an $80,000 painting for her birthday. She claimed it was a gift and he claimed it was an investment and therefore should be treated as marital property. In this case, the judge could have deemed that it was an investment. Because it was not the type of thing that most people would freely give as a gift, it was seen as an investment for the family so it was considered marital property. But remember that you can never predict what the judge will decide!

What happens when both parties want the same item? Let's say Beth and her husband had divided all their property except for one item. They couldn't agree on who would get the set of antique English crystal. They both wanted it so badly that they ended up spending $60,000 in court to decide that one issue. It seems absurd, but it happens every day. One of your roles as a financial planner is to insert reason and logic. At $60,000, they could have each bought a set and a trip to England!

Most often, the home furnishings are not included on the list of assets because the couple just divides the items. If they are to be valued, the typical value is what you can get from a garage sale.

## HOW WILL PROPERTY BE DIVIDED?

Martha and Tom have been married for 35 years. She stayed home and took care of the four children. Tom earns $150,000 per year and has started a business in the basement of their home, which he expects will bring in revenues after he retires from the corporation he works for. They own their home, which is worth $135,000. It is paid off. Tom's pension has been valued at $90,000. They have a savings account with $28,000, and he values the business at $75,000. Their assets total $328,000. Assuming a 50/50 property split, each would receive $164,000.

These are their assets:

| | |
|---|---|
| House | $135,000 |
| Pension | 90,000 |
| Savings | 28,000 |
| Business | 75,000 |
| Total | $328,000 |

However, splitting the property and assets down the middle is often not the most equitable division. In this case, as in nearly all divorces, Martha wants the house. It is not unusual for the wife to have an emotional attachment to the house, especially if that is where she raised the children. (For more information on deciding who gets the house, see Chapter 5.) For the remainder of this example, let's agree that Martha wants the house. So it goes into her column on a typical property settlement worksheet.

While women often have an emotional attachment to the house, men have emotional attachments to their pensions. Tom is no exception—he wants it all. We put the pension in his column.

Tom also says, "I have a business deal coming up soon and I am going to need cash for that deal. I must have the savings account." Put the savings account in his column. Then Tom says, "The business in the basement is mine. You don't know what it looks like and you don't even have an idea of what I do." Put the business in his column.

Here's what the division looks like.

| | | Her | Him |
|---|---|---|---|
| House | $135,000 | $135,000 | |
| Pension | 90,000 | | $ 90,000 |
| Savings | 28,000 | | 28,000 |
| Business | 75,000 | | 75,000 |
| Total | $328,000 | $135,000 | $193,000 |

Her assets total $135,000 and his assets total $193,000. If we were to look at a 50/50 property split, he would owe her $29,000. Although Tom has a large income of $150,000 a year, he does not want to give up any of the business, pension, or savings.

We can even out this division with a property settlement note. Tom can pay Martha $29,000 over time, like he would pay a note at the bank.

He can make monthly payments with current market interest. Or he can borrow funds directly from the bank since he has assets, including a savings account comparable to what he would owe.

## Property Settlement Note

A property settlement note is from the payer to the payee for an agreed-upon length of time with reasonable interest. It is still considered division of property, so the payer does not deduct it from taxable income. The payee does not pay taxes on the principal—only on the interest. It is important to collateralize this note. If there is no other asset available, it is possible to collateralize this note with a qualified pension by using a qualified domestic relations order (QDRO). If the payor defaults on the payments of a property settlement note, then the payee can start collecting pursuant to the terms of the QDRO agreement from the pension. (See Chapter 6 on pensions.)

Let's go back to Martha and Tom. Martha does not like this settlement. She says, "I want the house and I want half of your pension. We've been married for 35 years and I helped you earn that pension—I want half of that." Place the house's $135,000 value in her column and $45,000 of the pension in each column. Then she says, "I want half of the savings account. You're not going to leave me without any cash." Put $14,000 in her column and $14,000 in Tom's column. She agrees that the business is Tom's, so $75,000 is placed in his column. The property split now looks like this:

|  |  | Her | Him |
| --- | --- | --- | --- |
| House | $135,000 | $135,000 | |
| Pension | 90,000 | 45,000 | $ 45,000 |
| Savings | 28,000 | 14,000 | 14,000 |
| Business | 75,000 | | 75,000 |
| Total | $328,000 | $194,000 | $134,000 |

Her assets are valued at $194,000, his at $134,000. Martha owes Tom $30,000 to make a 50/50 property settlement. But it's not that simple. She does not have a job, has arthritis, and cannot walk very well. In reality, Martha is not in good health and is unlikely to get a job that pays above the minimum wage.

Her largest asset is the house, an illiquid asset. It is paid for, but it does not create revenues to buy groceries. She could rent out rooms for additional income, but that rarely works and it creates a different lifestyle that may be dissatisfactory to her. How is she going to pay this $30,000 to him? Given that the prospects for this are bleak, Martha and Tom's attorneys need to take another try at dividing the assets.

## Equal vs. Equitable

Property divisions can be likened to trading. You trade assets back and forth until the couple agrees on the division. In an equitable property division state, this means splitting the property equitably. Equitable does not always mean equal—it means fair.

On the other hand, the word *equality* suggests fairness and equity for all parties involved. However, the required equal division of property in most states has forced sales of family assets, especially the family

> **Equitable = Fair, not equal**

home, so that the proceeds can be divided between the two spouses. The net result is increased dislocation and disruption, especially in the lives of minor children. This is not fair in that the needs and interests of the children are not considered in many cases.

A second problem of equality is that a 50/50 division of property may not produce equal results—or equal standards of living after the divorce—if the two spouses are unequally situated at the time of divorce. This is most evident in the situation of the older homemaker. After a marital life devoted to homemaking, she is typically without substantial skills and experience in the workplace. Most likely, she will require a greater share of the property to cushion the income loss she suffers at divorce. Rarely is she in an equal economic position at divorce.

Generally, a 50/50 division is started when property is divided in an equitable division state. A major consideration can be how much separate property the client has. Let's say a client is fortunate enough to have $2 million in separate property. The marital estate totals $200,000. If the judge knows your client is walking out with $2 million of separate property, he or she may not give the client 50 percent of the marital property. Instead, the judge's attitude may be, "Well, you have $2 million in separate property so you get none of the marital property." That might seem equitable to the judge.

For help, you may want to consider software such as Divorce Plan™, which looks at the long-term results of any given settlement. It graphically and numerically illustrates where each party stands financially when certain assumptions are used. For instance, if the charts show that the wife runs out of assets within eight years while the husband is becoming very wealthy, it may indicate an adjustment is needed in the divorce settlement agreement. It's important to throw in a caveat here. When factoring in assumptions, the what-ifs must be realistic for your (and your client's) credibility.

## CAREER ASSETS

With many couples, one spouse has significant assets tied to his or her career. These career assets include insurance (life, health, and disability), vacation and sick pay, Social Security and unemployment benefits, stock options, and pension and retirement plans. Such things as future promotions, job experience, seniority, professional contacts, and education are also considered career assets. (For more information on pensions, insurance, and Social Security, see Chapters 6, 10, and 11.)

In many cases, career assets should be considered in arriving at an equitable settlement. For example, take a family in which the husband is the sole wage earner. Many times, the wife put the husband through school or helped him become established, abandoning or postponing her own education in the process. She may have quit her job to move from job to job with him. Together they have made the decision to spend the time and energy to build his career training with the expectation that she will share in the fruits of her investment through her husband's enhanced earning power. Over time, he has built up career assets which are part of what he earns even though they may not be paid out directly to him.

Even in two-income families, one spouse's career (usually the husband's) often takes priority. Both spouses expect to share the rewards of that decision—at least, in the beginning of their marriage.

Some states even place a value on degrees such as medical, dental, and law degrees. In a 1980 case, two premed students got married. The couple agreed that the husband would finish his education first while the wife supported him. When he finished, she would then complete her education. After his first year of residency, the couple separated. The court held that the husband's medical school degree and license to practice medicine were both obtained during the marriage, and therefore were "property" and were to be considered assets to be divided. It established the value of the husband's medical education as the difference in earning capacity between a man with a four-year college degree and a specialist in internal medicine. With the help of a financial analyst, the court valued the education at $306,000. The wife was awarded, in addition to alimony, 20 percent of this amount over a five-year period.[2]

A 1982 case in Wisconsin called on an economist to establish the value of the wife's investment in her husband's medical degree after a short marriage. The economist valued the degree in two different ways. The first method looked at what the wife actually paid for his tuition, books, and so on, coming up with $25,000. The second method compared the husband's earning potential in that area of the country as a white male over a 25-year period, both with and without his medical degree. The difference ($624,000) was brought back to present value using two different discount rates.

In this case, surprisingly, the wife asked for the $25,000 which she thought represented the value of her support. The court granted it, saying, "Both parties sacrificed so that he could become a doctor. In a sense, his medical degree is the most significant asset of the marriage. It is only fair that she be compensated for her costs and foregone opportunities resulting from her support of her husband while he was in school."[3]

## THE FAMILY BUSINESS

If one of the marital assets in a divorce is a business, there are often challenges in dividing this asset. A business can be anything from dentistry, medicine, or law to real estate or a home-based business. It can be a sole proprietorship, a partnership, or a corporation.

## Value the Business

Becky and James were getting a divorce after 35 years of marriage. James owned a heavy construction business. He agreed to split the assets 50/50 and said that the CPA at work valued the business at $300,000. Becky told her attorney, "I used to keep the books in the business for James, and we took in more than $1 million each year. Do you think it would only be worth $300,000?"

---

2. *Lynn v. Lynn,* 49 U.S.L.W. 2402 (N.J. Super. Ct., December 30, 1980).
3. *In re Marriage of Lundberg,* 107 Wis. 2d 1, 318 N.W.2d 918, 920 (1982).

Fortunately, Becky's attorney insisted that she have the business appraised. The appraisal cost Becky $4,300—she was very nervous to spend so much money. But the appraisal valued the company at $850,000 so her investment of $4,300 netted her $275,000 more than she would have received with the $300,000 valuation!

In a divorce situation, it is almost mandatory to have the business appraised. Becky was right to question the value of the business when it was figured by the CPA at her husband's business. There are certified business appraisers (CBAs) who value businesses. To earn this designation, appraisers must pass a rigorous written exam and submit appraisals for review by a committee of experienced peers.

## Divide the Business

There are three options when deciding how to divide the business. Either one spouse keeps the business, both spouses keep the business, or they sell the business outright.

### One Spouse Keeps the Business

In Becky and James' case, it was clear that the business was run by James and he would keep the business and buy out Becky's interest or give her other assets of equal value. If there are no assets large enough to give her, they could write up a property settlement note and he would pay her over time. If Becky owned shares of the company, the company could buy back her shares over time.

However, care needs to be taken when buying out shares of stock. If there has been an increase in the value of the stock, Becky could be liable for capital gains tax. If James bought her shares directly, it would be considered a transfer of property "incident to divorce," which is not a taxable issue. The basis would go with the stocks and would not be recognized until the stocks were sold by Becky later on.

### Both Continue to Work in the Business

On the other hand, it is much more difficult to divide a family-owned business where the husband and wife have worked next to each other every day for years. They both have emotional ties with the business. In addition, trying to divide the business may kill the business. Some couples are better business partners than marriage partners and so can continue to work together in a business after the divorce is final. However, this won't work for everyone!

## Sell the Business

Another option is to sell the business and divide the profits. This way, both parties are free to look elsewhere for another business or even to retire. The problem here may be in finding a buyer. It sometimes takes years to sell a business. In the meantime, until the business is sold, decisions need to be made as to whose business it is and who runs it.

Stella and Dan owned a national-franchise fast-food business. They also owned the land and the building the business was in. They had worked hard on this business together to make it a success. When they divorced, they finally made the difficult decision that Dan would take the business and Stella would take the land and building. This decision made Stella the landlord, which allowed her to control the rent that the business paid her and also to decide how repairs and maintenance on the building should be handled. They soon realized they had made a bad decision. It cost them more money with their attorneys to hammer out a new buyout agreement that allowed Dan to keep the business and the property, and gave Stella enough cash to move out of the area and start over in a new location.

## HIDDEN ASSET CHECKLIST

The divorce process is a time of mistrust for each spouse. Rightly or wrongly, each may accuse the other of hiding assets.

If you find hidden assets, they can be used as a smoking gun. Revealing your discovery of them early in the case may encourage rapid settlement. But if the personalities of the parties are likely to stand in the way of settlement, then reveal them during the trial. This evidence will be a big blow to the credibility of the party hiding the assets.

> Assets are traditionally hidden in one of four ways. The person either denies the existence of an asset, transfers it to a third party, claims offset (which means the asset exists but was diverted), or claims the asset was lost or dissipated. In addition to these, there is a new way to hide assets: creation of false debt.

Tax returns are the first place to start in discovery to find assets. (*Discovery* is the process during which both sides in the case share documents and financial information before the case goes to court.) It's a good idea to go back five years. Perusal of tax returns can help your client, especially if they reveal things about which your client was unaware. The first two pages of a tax return can serve as a table of contents, since they identify all the schedules and additional attachments to the basic return.

Several forms are important to review:

Schedule B (interest and dividend deductions) may identify assets in detail.

Schedule C (business or professional income) offers the chance for game playing and a place to hide assets.

Schedule D reports gains and losses from stocks, bonds, and real estate.

Schedule E shows certain business interests.

Form 1065 reports partnership returns.

Form 1120 reports corporate returns.

Form 2119 covers the sale of a residence.

Form 2441 claims child care expenses.

You want to review both federal and state tax returns, and compare them to all 1099s and W2s. Amended returns may also make a difference. And remember, your last question in a deposition should be "Is there any income not shown on your tax return?"

The following information is excerpted from *The Divorce Handbook* by James T. Friedman, a valuable resource for financial planners assisting their clients during a divorce. Mr. Friedman is a specialist in family law. Since 1970 he has been regularly engaged in drafting family-law–related legislation on behalf of the Illinois State Bar Association, the Chicago Bar Association, and the American Academy of Matrimonial Lawyers.[4]

*     *     *     *

In the course of discovery (sharing documents and financial information with the opposing side), most spouses believe that their counterpart has

---

4. James T. Friedman, *The Divorce Handbook* Chapter 7 ("Financial Hide-and-Seek with Your Spouse"). (New York: Random House, 1982, 1984) pp. 49–53.

somehow hidden or failed to disclose the existence of certain assets. The following checklist of items to research may assist in determining the whereabouts of hidden assets or whether, in fact, they exist at all.

**1.** *Financial statements:* Any loans from lending institutions require sworn financial statements to be filled out. In most cases, the borrower is trying to impress the lending institution with the extent of assets and may exaggerate these. Looking back five years or so at these statements may put you on the trail of assets that are now unaccounted for, or that show valuations substantially greater than what is now claimed.

**2.** *Personal income-tax returns:* A review of the personal returns filed during the past five years may indicate sources of interest or dividends. The returns may also reveal unknown sources of income or loss from trusts, partnerships, or real estate holdings.

**3.** *Corporate tax returns:* If one spouse is the principal owner of a closely held corporation, he or she may be manipulating salary by taking loans from the corporation. Or he or she may be charging personal expenses to corporate accounts, which will later be reimbursed or charged to the officer's loan account. Corporate returns should also be checked for excessive or unnecessary retained earnings (undistributed profits). These may disguise available profit distributions or an artificially low salary level. Reimbursement of prior capital contributions or repayments of loans to the corporation may also provide hidden cash flow to your spouse.

**4.** *Partnership returns:* The comparison of partnership returns (IRS Forms 1065 and K1) over the years when the returns are available will indicate any sudden changes in the partnership interest or distribution. Such changes often occur at the time of a divorce and then compensating adjustments are made after the divorce is completed.

**5.** *Canceled checks and check registers from personal, partnership, and closed corporation accounts:* While time-consuming, it is always revealing to go over all the canceled checks and bank statements from personal accounts for the past few years, and post the expenditures to different columns under utilities, entertainment, loan payments, and so on. You will learn the amount of total expenditures per year, which sometimes exceeds income, and you will have a better feeling for cost of living and where budget cuts should be made. In terms of hidden assets, you may come across canceled checks for expenditures for the purchase or maintenance of property that you never knew existed. It is important to check the canceled checks against the appropriate bank statement to make sure that you have all of the canceled checks. It is possible that certain checks were removed before they were delivered to you.

**6.** *Savings account passbooks:* Acquire the passbooks for any savings accounts open during the past five years or more. Look for any deposits or withdrawals that are unusual in amount or in pattern. A monthly withdrawal or deposit of money in the same odd amount may reflect mortgage payments or income receipts from sources that you are not aware of.

**7.** *Securities or commodities account statements:* If one spouse has been buying and selling stocks or bonds or dealing in commodities, the broker with whom he or she trades furnishes monthly or quarterly statements indicating all transactions. A review of these statements going back a few years could reveal the existence of securities of which there was no knowledge or could raise questions as to the disposition of stock sales proceeds. Cross-checking securities transactions and bank accounts by date and amount will usually verify the source or disposition of the monies involved. If the securities are sold and the proceeds are unaccounted for, you can be sure the money's out there somewhere.

**8.** *Expense account abuse:* Very often, a corporate employer will allow employees a great deal of leeway in their expense-account reporting. A spouse may take advantage of this by exaggerating or even falsifying business expenditures. The employer maintains records as to expense account disbursements to the employee over the year with monthly detail. A check of these records will indicate the extent to which the employee is able to "live off" the expense account. A cross-check between expense account disbursements and savings account or checking account deposits may indicate a pattern of expense account abuse if the deposits exceed legitimate business expenditures.

**9.** *Deferred salary increase, uncollected bonus, or commissions:* It is always a good idea to check directly by subpoena or otherwise with the spouse's employer to determine whether a salary increase is overdue, when it will be forthcoming, and how much it is. Employers are sometimes sympathetic to their divorcing employees and so are willing to bend the rules slightly to defer salary increases, bonuses, or commissions in order to suppress apparent income. Ultimately, these increases, bonuses, or commissions must be paid to keep the corporate books straight, and the employer will rarely lie when put under oath or forced to make a written statement on the subject. Sympathy goes just so far.

**10.** *Safe-deposit-box activity:* The bank that maintains the safe-deposit box keeps records of who enters the box and when. These records will not indicate contents of a box or what, if anything, has been removed. If the first spouse was aware of the contents at the point when the records indicate the second spouse opened the box and something is now missing, he or she has a pretty good idea of who took it.

**11.** *Cash transaction and in-kind compensation:* One spouse may be a physician or a shopkeeper, or be in some other work where cash is paid, or he or she may receive in-kind compensation, where something of value—other than cash—is given in exchange for services. Such cash payments or noncash items are rarely reported on the income-tax return, but if you know of such income in the past and can subpoena current information, it will help in proving available income in excess of that shown on the income-tax returns. If one spouse buys things of substantial value with cash, there is probably a source of cash income somewhere. Most people don't retain cash in a noninterest-bearing form unless they're hiding its source.

**12.** *Children's bank accounts:* Frequently, a spouse who wishes to hide money will open a custodial account in the name of a child. Deposits and withdrawals are made without any intent that the child have use of the account except in case of the spouse's death. The interest from these accounts is not shown on income-tax returns, nor are returns filed for the children.

**13.** *Personal knowledge of spouse's habits:* One of the most useful discovery tools is personal knowledge of the spouse's habits with money. People who are attempting to hide money very seldom do so without making some form of written note so they can have a personal account of what they have done. When things are going well in a marriage, the spouse may tell the other spouse about such records, but you can be sure they will disappear in case of divorce. The more secretive a person is, the more detailed such notes are likely to be. If a spouse has neglected to declare income to the IRS, the knowledge of hidden income or assets may prove to be a powerful leverage factor in reaching a satisfactory settlement.

**14.** *Phony income-tax returns:* When the divorce has been filed, some spouses are inclined to alter the copies of their previously filed income-tax returns to hide or adjust pertinent financial information. If you have reason to believe that furnished copies have been altered, ask for copies of jointly filed returns directly from the Internal Revenue Service.

**15.** *Phony loans or debts:* To keep cash from being divided, a spouse may sometimes attempt to bury the money with a phony loan to a cooperative friend or relative. The loan may be tied up with a long-term note or with a claimed likelihood of uncollectibility, so as to remove this money from consideration at settlement time. The other spouse, who was never aware of the debt, of course did not sign the note because it probably came into existence *after* the divorce proceedings commenced. Sudden payment of debts to out-of-state creditors who are not available for deposition is usually a sign that the debt is a phony.

**16.** *"Friends" or other phonies on the payroll:* If one spouse is in a position to control the payroll of a sole proprietorship, partnership, or closely held corporation, he or she may be paying salaries to a friend or relative who is not actually providing services commensurate with the compensation. The friend on the payroll may be stashing the money away or they may be both enjoying it currently. In either case, the profit of the enterprise will be reduced accordingly and your spouse may be drawing a lesser salary. The same ploy can be used for payment to phony independent contractors.

**17.** *Retirement-plan abuse:* If one spouse has established a pension or profit-sharing plan in connection with a closely held corporation, the plan should be carefully checked to determine whether monies that have been contributed to the account are being invested in accordance with the plan requirements. Very often, deductions will be taken for contributions to such plans, and then the money is used for personal living expenses or taken out as loans that are never repaid.

**18.** *Defined-benefit pension plans:* Defined-benefit pension plans are distinguished from defined-contribution plans by the fact that the *benefits* payable at retirement age are specified within the plan itself rather than by some contribution formula. The amount of the contributions then must be actuarially determined, based on the age of the intended beneficiary and the point at which benefits are to be paid. A great deal of income can be buried by substantial payments into such a plan during the years preceding or during divorce litigation. The required payments can be a substantial portion of the beneficiary's income if that is what is required to achieve the defined goal at retirement. This, of course, leaves little money available for support or division as marital property. Once the divorce is completed, the defined-benefit plan can be discarded, even though a substantial tax loss may result.

**19.** *Gift and inheritance tax returns:* Much useful information is available from inheritance, estate, or gift-tax returns of relatives you believe have been generous to the spouse. If these returns show that there were substantial gifts or bequests that have not been accounted for in the settlement negotiations, you are alerted that other assets could also be hidden. A tracing will have to be made from the estate's distribution to see what has happened to the assets.

*     *     *     *

Now that we've looked at different kinds of property, how to find it, and how to divide it, it is time to address the most common piece of property in a divorce—the house.

## CHAPTER 5

# Dividing the House

In many divorces, the biggest question is who gets the house. Should the wife get it, should the husband, or should they sell it and split the profit (if there is one)? Often the answer isn't easy or clear.

Many times, the wife has an emotional tie to the house and she wants to keep it. This is where she raised the children and decorated and entertained. Her whole life revolved around this house. Unfortunately, she does not stop to think about the value of that asset. If it is almost paid off and has a lot of equity in it, she is getting an illiquid asset that does not buy groceries for her children or create any income.

## THREE BASIC OPTIONS

There are three basic options to approaching the issue of who gets the house: to sell the house, to have one spouse buy out the other spouse's half, or to have both exspouses continue to own the property jointly.

## Sell the House

Selling the house and dividing the profits that remain after sales costs and the mortgage are paid off is the easiest and most "clean" way of dividing equity. Concerns to be addressed include the basis and possible capital gains (addressed later in this chapter), buying another house versus renting, being able to qualify for a new loan, and the over-age-55 exclusion.

## Buy Out the Other Spouse

Buying out the other spouse's half works if one person wants to remain in the house or wants to own the house, but there are difficulties with this option that need to be considered.

First of all, a value of the property needs to be agreed to. This is the equity in the house. Next, decide on the dollar amount of the buyout. Will the dollar amount have subtracted from it selling costs and capital gains taxes (in case the owner needs to sell it sooner than expected)?

Then a method of payment needs to be selected. If there is a time period where the payment occurs, the terms need to be comfortable for both parties. The payment could be as simple as giving up another marital asset in trade for the equity in the house. The house could be refinanced to withdraw cash to pay the other spouse, or a note payable could be drawn up with terms of payment agreeable to both parties. In the case of a note, there should be reasonable interest attached to it and it should be collateralized with a deed of trust on the property. A problem with this arrangement is that it keeps the exspouses in an uncomfortable debtor–creditor relationship.

There is another problem with buying out the other spouse's half. Let's say the wife gets the house and both names are on the deed. The husband can quitclaim the deed to her so that only her name is on the deed. She can sell it whenever she wants to. Although his name comes off the deed, it remains on the mortgage. He is still liable if she decides to quit making the payments. The mortgage company doesn't care if they are divorced or not. The only way he can get his name off the mortgage is for her to assume the loan, refinance it, or pay it off. When the husband's name is kept on the mortgage, this may impact his credit. He could be viewed as overextended unless he has proof that she is making the mortgage payments. This continues what may be an adversarial relationship.

## Own the House Jointly

The other option—continuing to own the property jointly—is used by some couples when they want the children to stay in the house until they finish school, they reach a certain age, or the resident exspouse remarries or cohabits. The couple may agree to sell the house after the children have graduated from school; they may split the proceeds evenly. The one who stays in the house in the meantime can pay the mortgage while all other costs of maintaining the house plus taxes and repairs can be split evenly. Again, this creates a tie between the exspouses that may cause stress.

To help put all these options into perspective, here are some examples. Mark and Susan both had very good jobs when they decided to divorce in 1986. Susan wanted to stay in the house with the three children and buy out Mark's half of the house with a property settlement note. Interest rates were high. The note was drawn with her agreeing to pay him his half of the equity at 14 percent interest. Then property values began to decline. Susan's half of the equity was losing value; his half was earning 14 percent, even after the interest rates plummeted. Nobody presumed at the time they drew up this agreement that interest rates or property values were going to go down. It is always a risk when you do agreements that extend out into the future. These risks run both ways.

Lila and Keith had divided all their property with her owing him $5,000. She kept the house and she was going to sell it in three years when their daughter was out of high school. The house had $20,000 of equity in it at the time of divorce. They both agreed that when she sold the house in three years, she would give him his $5,000. However, Lila's attorney knew Susan's lawyer and had heard about the case where Susan was paying 14 percent interest. Lila's attorney suggested, "Since $5,000 represents 25 percent of the equity, why don't you agree on a percentage? That way, when you sell the house you give him 25 percent of the profits. If the house declines in value and you only get $10,000 profit, you are not paying him half. Or if it goes up, you both win because you both get more."

If your client is talking about dividing assets beyond one year of the divorce, talk about percentages versus exact dollars. If the talk is about dividing assets prior to a year, specifying hard dollars usually works. But further in the future, it is much safer and much wiser to talk percentages.

## BASIS

June and Stan are getting divorced and they have three assets: a cabin on a lake worth $190,000, a 401(k) plan worth $90,000 and a certificate of deposit worth $140,000. Stan said, "Why don't you take the cabin and sell it?" He had borrowed $140,000 against the cabin a year before, and put the money into a CD, which she was aware of. "If you sell it, you will get $50,000. "You take the 401(k) worth $90,000, and I'll take the CD, so we each end up with $140,000."

June talked this over with her attorney and they thought that this sounded fair.

| Assets | | June | Stan |
|---|---|---|---|
| Cabin | $190,000 | | |
| | −140,000 | | |
| | 50,000 | $50,000 | |
| 401(k) | 90,000 | 90,000 | |
| CD | 140,000 | | $140,000 |
| Total | $280,000 | $140,000 | $140,000 |

What Stan did not talk about—and what the attorney should have asked about—was the basis in the cabin. Stan had paid $20,000 for this cabin 15 years earlier. There was a $170,000 capital gain, which created a tax of $56,100 (capital gains tax at 28 percent plus state tax at 5 percent). June received $50,000 and had to pay out $56,100, so she was out-of-pocket another $6,100.

| | |
|---|---|
| Capital gain | $170,000 |
| | |
| Federal tax (28%) | 47,600 |
| State tax (5%) | 8,500 |
| Total capital gains tax | $ 56,100 |

The after-tax value of the 401(k) plan was approximately $60,300, so June ended up with $54,200. The $140,000 that Stan borrowed from the cabin and put in the CD was his, tax-free and clear. He ended up with $140,000 and she ended up with $54,200, because the question was not asked about the basis. Do you think June's attorney had some liability here? Absolutely!

| Assets | | June | Stan |
|---|---|---|---|
| Cabin | $ (6,100) | $(6,100) | |
| 401(k) | 60,300 | 60,300 | |
| CD | 140,000 | | $140,000 |
| Total | | $54,200 | $140,000 |

After being involved with over 600 divorce cases, I find that the one question most overlooked by attorneys is, What is the basis in the house (or stocks, other real estate, or other investments in the couple's portfolio)?

## FROM THE CPA'S POINT OF VIEW

There are many challenges with the different variations on the theme of basis and capital gains. Gail Heinzman (a CPA in Boulder, Colorado, with more than 15 years of tax experience in public accounting and in corporate settings) was asked to test our knowledge with some case studies, and had the following to say.

*     *     *     *

In most divorces, the couple's most valuable asset is their house. Questions arise whether to keep it or sell it. If they plan to keep it, who is going to keep it? How will the house be valued for the settlement? If it is going to be sold, when will it be sold? Is it going to be sold before or after the divorce? The tax implications of these questions are usually overlooked until well after the divorce. As a result, the sale of the home can result in unforeseen income tax liabilities.

The following two cases discuss the tax implications of scenarios often encountered in divorce and new-relationship situations. While these cases are not exhaustive, they illustrate some of the tax pitfalls relating to home sales often encountered while ending a marriage and other tax difficulties that may arise when entering into a new relationship. Relatively minor changes in facts can significantly affect the tax results of home sale transactions. Care should be taken to thoroughly understand and document the specifics of each case.

## Case 1

Steve and Linda have been married for several years. They purchased their first home (home 1) years ago and sold it in 1989 when their youngest child went to college. They purchased their second house (home 2) two months before the sale of their first house. The information relating to these homes is summarized below.

|                           | Home 1   | Home 2    |
| ------------------------- | -------- | --------- |
| Purchase price            | $45,000  | $180,000  |
| Improvements              | 10,000   | 12,000    |
| Real estate commissions   | 6,000    | 9,000     |
| Mortgage balance at sale  | 15,000   | 130,000   |
| Gross proceeds            | 150,000  | 230,000   |

## Question I
What was their basis in the second house?

|                                    | Home 1    | Home 2    |                  |
| ---------------------------------- | --------- | --------- | ---------------- |
| Purchase price                     | $ 45,000  | $180,000  |                  |
| Improvements                       | 10,000    | 12,000    |                  |
| Gain carried over from prior residence |       | (89,000)  |                  |
| Total basis                        | $ 55,000  | $103,000  |                  |
|                                    |           |           |                  |
| Selling price                      | 150,000   | 230,000   | *These facts are* |
| Expenses of sale                   | 6,000     | 9,000     | *relevant later* |
| Net selling price                  | $144,000  | $221,000  | *in this case.*  |
|                                    |           |           |                  |
| Realized gain (loss) on sale       | 89,000    |           |                  |
| Net deferred gain                  | $ 89,000  |           |                  |

The original house was purchased for $45,000. They completed improve-
ments of $10,000; thus, their basis in home 1 was $55,000. The mortgage
balance is irrelevant for determining basis despite its impact on the cash
that the couple will receive at sale. Home 1 was sold for $150,000, but
there were commissions and closing costs of $6,000, so the net proceeds
are $144,000.

Their gain is computed by subtracting their basis ($55,000) from
their net proceeds ($144,000). The gain from the sale of home 1 was
$89,000. They purchased home 2 for $180,000. Because the purchase
price of home 2 exceeded the net proceeds from the sale of home 1, the
entire $89,000 gain is deferred. Steve and Linda recognized no gain on
the sale of home 1 in 1989.

After the purchase of home 2, Steve and Linda added $12,000 of
improvements to the property. Therefore, they invested $192,000 in home
2 between the purchase price and improvements. However, this number
is not their basis in the property. Their basis must be adjusted downward
for the deferred gain of $89,000 from home 1. Their basis in their second
house is not $192,000 but $103,000 ($192,000 minus $89,000 of deferred gain). It is against the $103,000 that the taxable gain would be
computed for home 2.

Often, when a couple has been married for an extended period of
time and have owned several homes, they have no idea of what the
basis is in their house. They assume, "We bought it for $180,000 and
we built a deck on the back for $12,000, so we've paid $192,000 for the
house." They forget about their previous house or series of houses over
the years.

Using this logic, Steve estimated the potential gain on their home to be $35,000 to $40,000. When the numbers are crunched, the actual gain is $127,000 on the sale of the second house.

Knowing these facts is critical to deciding whether the client should keep or sell the house. The party keeping the house must understand the often hidden deferred tax liability he or she is assuming if keeping the house is part of the divorce settlement.

## Question 2

What if home 2 was sold for $170,000?

This amount is less than Steve and Linda's purchase price of $180,000. However, the selling price still exceeds their basis of $103,000; there is a tax gain of $67,000 ( i.e., $170,000 minus $103,000) even though they sold it for less than its purchase price. The gain would be deferred or recognized depending on their reinvestment choices.

## Question 3

What if home 2 were sold for $102,000?

This amount is less than Steve and Linda's purchase price of the home and less than their basis. They would experience an economic loss on the sale. However, they would not receive a tax benefit for the loss because losses on sale of a personal residence are not deductible.

## Question 4

Instead of selling home 2 at a loss, assume the couple sold home 1 at a loss. How would the order of the loss affect their tax liability at divorce?

As noted above, there is no tax deduction for selling a personal residence for a loss. The couple's basis in home 2 would not be affected by the loss. Therefore, their basis in home 2 would be its purchase price plus improvements, or $192,000.

## Question 5

Referring back to the facts of Question 1, Steve and Linda were divorced and sold home 2 in 1994. Linda bought a new condominium for $175,000 later that year. Steve decided to rent until 1997, when he will receive a significant trust distribution from his family. Then he plans to spend $500,000 on a house. Is anyone liable for tax on the gain from the sale of home 2? If so, in what tax year is the gain recognized?

## COMMON ISSUES IN DETERMINING BASIS

### FORM 2119

The Internal Revenue Service requires that its Form 2119, ("Sale of Your Home"), be completed and attached to an income tax return each time that an individual sells a house. This form is mandatory whether or not there was gain recognized on the sale. If available, this form should state the couple's basis in their current residence. However, if the couple prepared their own tax returns, this form is often omitted or completed incorrectly. A brief discussion with the client and/or tax preparer may be advisable.

### WHAT IS AN IMPROVEMENT?

Homeowners incur many costs to maintain and improve their homes. Maintenance costs do not increase the tax basis of the home, but improvements do. If the client estimates that a substantial amount of money was spent on improvements, request a list of the improvements. Have an accountant review the list to help clarify whether the "improvements" meet the IRS definition.

### SUMMARY OF BASIS ISSUES

When people estimate their equity in a home, they evaluate it from an economic rather than a tax perspective. The two are seldom the same. Be sure to get copies of the couple's Forms 2119 from prior residences or take whatever other steps are necessary to understand the magnitude of their deferred gains if the residence is sold.

A taxpayer must reinvest in a new principal residence within two years before or after sale. Here, Linda would meet these requirements, but Steve would not.

|  | Home 1 | Home 2 | Linda's Condo |
|---|---|---|---|
| Purchase price | $ 45,000 | $180,000 | $175,000 |
| Improvements | 10,000 | 12,000 |  |
| Gain carried over from prior residence |  | (89,000) | (59,000) |
| Total basis | $ 55,000 | $103,000 | $116,000 |
|  |  |  |  |
| Selling price | 150,000 | 230,000 |  |
| Expenses of sale | 6,000 | 9,000 |  |
| Net selling price | $144,000 | $221,000 |  |

| Realized gain (loss) on sale | $89,000 | $118,000 |
|---|---|---|
| Recognized gain by Steve | | 59,000 |
| Net deferred gain | $89,000 | $ 59,000 |

Under this option, Steve's gain is recognized.

In this case, both Steve and Linda have a two-year window both before and after the date of sale to reinvest their shares of the net proceeds from the sale in order to defer this gain. If Steve reinvests his half of the sales proceeds in 1997, he is outside of that window. Linda would have the opportunity to defer her portion of the gain, but Steve would not. Instead, he would have a taxable gain of $59,000 computed by subtracting his half of the basis of $103,000 (or $51,500) from gross proceeds of $110,500. Steve's tax is due on his 1994 return, not on his 1996 return.

This provision can be a pitfall. Many people assume that the two-year window is a tax deferral as well as an investment deferral; it is not. The sale of the house is the event creating the gain and that event occurred in 1994. If Steve misses the reinvestment window, he must amend his 1994 tax return and must pay the tax plus interest as well as any penalties levied by the IRS or state. Gains from the sale of a home are usually taxed as capital gains, which are currently subject to a maximum tax rate of 28 percent.

If a client is not sure he or she is going to replace a home, it may make sense to pay the tax to avoid the penalties and interest. If reinvestment occurs, the prior year's income tax return can be amended and the tax overpayment can be refunded. A practical issue is whether the client has the money to pay the tax, make a subsequent down payment, and qualify for the mortgage if the decision is subsequently made to reinvest.

## Question 6

Now assume the same facts as in Question 5 except that Steve and Linda's divorce was final in February 1995. Now who is liable for tax? In what tax year is the gain recognized?

Since they were not divorced in the year of sale, the tax implications are not clear. Taxpayers could treat the transaction either as outlined in Question 5 or as outlined below.

| | Home 1 | Home 2 | Linda's Condo |
|---|---|---|---|
| Purchase price | $45,000 | $180,000 | $175,000 |
| Improvements | 10,000 | 12,000 | |
| Gain carried over from prior residence | | (89,000) | (72,000) |
| Total basis | $55,000 | $103,000 | $103,000 |

| | | |
|---|---:|---:|
| Selling price | $150,000 | $230,000 |
| Expenses of sale | 6,000 | 9,000 |
| Net selling price | $144,000 | $221,000 |
| | | |
| Realized gain (loss) on sale | $ 89,000 | $118,000 |
| Recognized gain by Steve and Linda | | 46,000 |
| Net deferred gain | $ 89,000 | $ 72,000 |

Under this option, tax is minimized but the entire deferred tax liability is absorbed by Linda. However, both Steve and Linda would be liable for the tax if they each filed a joint tax return for 1994. If the settlement requires Steve to pay the tax on this gain, Linda could file a separate return to avoid any audit liability.

## Question 7

Linda wants to keep the house, but Steve wants his share of the equity to start a new life. All other pieces of the property settlement have been agreed to. Steve's attorney proposes that Linda pay Steve $115,000 in cash and liquid investments to buy him out of the house. The house is paid off so there is no mortgage. What would Linda's basis in the house be when she sells the house if she accepts this proposal?

Linda's basis in the house would not be affected by the proposed payment to Steve. Her basis in the house would continue to be $103,000 even though she has given him $115,000 as part of the settlement. There is no adjustment to basis when property is split up as part of a divorce property settlement.

## Question 8

Assume that Linda and Steve divorce in 1994. Linda keeps home 2 but sells it in 1995 and buys the $175,000 condo. Will she have a gain to recognize? If so, how much?

Linda will recognize a gain to the extent of unreinvested proceeds.

| | Home 1 | Home 2 | Linda's Condo |
|---|---:|---:|---:|
| Purchase price | $ 45,000 | $180,000 | $175,000 |
| Improvements | 10,000 | 12,000 | |
| Gain carried over from prior residence | | (89,000) | (72,000) |
| Total basis | $ 55,000 | $103,000 | $103,000 |
| | | | |
| Selling price | 150,000 | 230,000 | |
| Expenses of sale | 6,000 | 9,000 | |
| Net selling price | $144,000 | $221,000 | |

| Net proceeds | | $221,000 |
| Amount reinvested | | 175,000 |
| Unreinvested proceeds | | $ 46,000 |
| | | |
| Realized gain (loss) on sale | $89,000 | $118,000 |
| Unreinvested proceeds | | 46,000 |
| Net deferred gain | $89,000 | $ 72,000 |

Since Linda kept the house pursuant to the property settlement, her basis is $103,000. Since she is not reinvesting the full amount of the net proceeds from the sale of home 2, she will need to recognize gain in the amount of the lesser of

> The gain realized on the sale or
>
> The amount of unreinvested proceeds.

In this example, the gain realized was $118,000, and the unreinvested proceeds were $46,000. Linda is liable for all the tax on the gain.

## Question 9

Assume that Steve was age 57 at the time of the divorce. Would this change your planning?

Subject to certain limitations, a taxpayer who is 55 years old or older may exclude one time up to $125,000 of gain on the sale of his principal residence. The term *a taxpayer* includes both the husband and wife if they file a joint return for the year the exclusion is claimed.

If Steve and Linda did not divorce until 1995 and filed jointly in 1994, they could permanently eliminate tax on the $46,000 gain. However, this approach would permanently eliminate both of their abilities to claim a future exclusion.

If they are married and file separately, Steve could eliminate $59,000 in gain, but Linda would lose her ability to claim any portion of a $125,000 exclusion in the future. This provision was introduced to preclude married couples from accruing two exclusions by filing separately.

The best tax result is to sell the house in the year after the divorce. Steve could exclude his gain and Linda would still be eligible to exclude gain up to $125,000 on the subsequent sale of a residence. Imagine the consequences of such as strategy. A new category for singles ads could be to put down whether you still have your exemption or not.

# Case 2

Jon and Margery are in their late thirties and have each been successful in their chosen careers. Each owns a home. They are planning to marry in the fall of 1994. The following table summarizes the information about their homes.

|  | Margery's Home | Jon's Home |
|---|---|---|
| Purchase price | $240,000 | $180,000 |
| Improvements | 10,000 | 12,000 |
| Real estate commissions | 12,000 | 9,000) |
| Fair market value | $300,000 | $230,000 |

Margery purchased her house for $240,000. She finished the basement for $10,000. The house has a fair market value today of $300,000 and the mortgage has been paid off. Jon purchased his for $180,000. With improvements of $12,000, it has a fair market value of $230,000. Jon moves into Margery's house in January 1994 and purchases a half interest in her house immediately so that he can take advantage of the interest in the tax writeoff. What are the tax implications to Margery?

Margery has a tax liability. She sold half of her principal residence and she cannot reinvest in another principal residence because she still lives in the same house. Margery's gain will be $19,000. Her gross proceeds will be $144,000 (i.e., $150,000 or half of the fair market value of the house, less $6,000 for half of the real estate commission). Her basis will be $125,000 (i.e., $120,000 or one half of the purchase price plus $5,000 for half of the improvements). Her gain of $19,000 is computed by subtracting the $125,000 basis from the $144,000 in net proceeds. The presence of a mortgage would further complicate this example, depending on whether Jon became liable for a portion of the mortgage.

\*     \*     \*     \*

## LOSING THE BENEFIT OF BUYING ANOTHER HOME IN TWO YEARS

If a person sells a principal residence and buys a new one within two years, the capital gain can be deferred or "rolled over" into the new home (under §1034 IRC).

One problem arises when a divorcing spouse moves out of the marital home before it's sold. He or she may lose the rollover provision because the home will no longer be his "principal residence" at the time of the sale. Since this is frequent, it's imperative that the lawyer and financial advisors make sure that both parties are aware of the IRS position.

If the house will be sold shortly after one of the spouses moves out, the problem may be avoided by maintaining ties between the spouse and the home and thus demonstrating an "intent to return." Courts have allowed spouses to use the rollover where they demonstrated this intent up until the time of the sale. Indications of this intent may include

Renting rather than buying after moving out.

Documenting in letters that the reason for moving out was solely to reduce emotional distress.

Continuing to receive mail at the home.

Leaving belongings there.

Performing routine maintenance.

Courts have also held that a spouse can use the rollover if the house was listed for sale before he or she moved out.

## LOSING THE "55 OR OVER" EXCLUSION

A person who is 55 or over can exclude up to $125,000 of gain from the sale of a principal residence under §121 of the Code. If your clients are eligible for this exclusion, you generally want to sell *after* the divorce.

If the sale occurs before the divorce, the couple can exclude a total of only $125,000 (or $62,500 each if filing separately). But if the sale occurs after the divorce is final, each spouse can use the full $125,000 exclusion. This is true even if only one of the spouses owns the house separately.

However, if one spouse owns the house separately and sells it before the divorce and takes the exclusion, the other spouse will be forever barred from using it. This won't be true if the sale occurs after the divorce.

Another consideration is that if the sale occurs before the divorce, both parties must consent to the use of the exclusion, even if only one spouse uses it. Thus, one spouse could block the other's tax planning.

A home is a "principal residence" under §121 if the spouse lived there for three of the past five years. This means that you usually don't have the "moving out" problem under §121 that you often have with the §1034 rollover.

If your clients can use the exclusion, advise them not to sell the home while they are still married. It's the worst possible thing to do. Unfortunately, many lawyers miss this timing issue entirely.

## WHEN THE WIFE *SHOULD* GET THE HOUSE

There are cases when the wife should keep the house, even when doing so will create an unequal settlement. Let's look at Bill and Barbara.

Bill and Barbara are 45 and 49, respectively, and have been married 18 years. They have one son, age 17. Bill earns $2,175 per month minus child support payments of $413. His living expenses are $1,400 per month, which leaves him with a surplus of $362 per month. Barbara earns $780 per month plus $413 child support. Her living expenses with the son are $1,630 per month, which creates a *negative* cash flow of $437 per month.

|  | Barbara | Bill |
|---|---|---|
| Take-home pay | $   780 | $2,175 |
| Living expenses | (1,630) | (1,400) |
| Child support | 413 | (413) |
| Cash flow | $  (437) | $   362 |

The following settlement was decided by the judge. Barbara will receive the house, which has equity of $44,100, and her IRA worth $5,000. Bill will get his IRA worth $8,900. There are no other assets. Since Barbara gets the house with $44,000 worth of equity, she has to pay Bill half of that equity upon the first of the following events: if she sells the house, if she remarries, or upon the emancipation of the child, which varies from state to state. We do not know if she is going to sell the house or remarry, but we do know that the son is going to turn 19 within two years.

Barbara's house payment is $290 per month with 10 years left on the mortgage. According to this scenario, Barbara is heading for poverty from the outset. To be able to pay Bill his half of the equity in the house, she will *have* to sell the house. This will force her to rent at a much higher cost than her house payment of $290 per month. In her area, rents start at $400 to $450 per month.

This court order is forcing Barbara into severe poverty. In this case, it seems reasonable that Barbara should have been allowed to keep the house without paying Bill half the equity—an unequal but equitable settlement.

## WHEN THE WIFE SHOULD *NOT* GET THE HOUSE

There are cases when the wife should not keep the house. The following example of Bob and Cindy illustrates in detail the financial pitfalls that can arise.

Cindy is 32 years old and Bob is 33. They have been married 12 years. Their two children—ages 9 and 5—will remain with Cindy. Bob is offering to pay $250 per month per child for child support.

Bob started his own business three years ago; he places a value of $200,000 on it. He argues that the business is so new that its value cannot be counted on and therefore should not be divided.

Cindy needs three more years of school to finish college. She will then be able to bring home about $17,000 per year. She will not be able to earn income while finishing school. Bob is offering to help Cindy through school by paying maintenance of $2,000 per month for one year and then $1,500 per month for two additional years.

Cindy's expenses with the two children are $4,020 per month. This includes her expenses for school, which average $350 per month. Bob earns $75,000 per year and brings home $57,570 per year. His expenses are $2,050 per month.

The family home has a fair market value (FMV) of $220,000 with a mortgage of $130,000 at 7.5 percent interest for 15 years. Monthly payments are $1,500 per month (principal, interest, taxes, and insurance). Cindy wants to remain in the house with the children.

They have a rental house worth $90,000 with a mortgage of $50,000. Rental income is $600 per month and the mortgage payment is $600 per month. Their IRAs total $17,000. They have credit card debt of $22,600.

Bob has made the following proposal called scenario 1. Cindy will take the house, the rental, the IRAs, and the debt. Bob will keep only his business.

This couple had trouble keeping within their budget while they were married. Cindy tended to overspend and thus increased their credit card debt. The challenge in this case will be counseling Cindy on the importance of staying within her budget.

Look at the asset table, Table 5–1. The net equity in the home, $90,000, is in Cindy's column. The net equity in the rental, $33,700, is in Cindy's column. The business is in Bob's column. The IRAs ($17,000) and debt ($22,600) are in Cindy's column. Let's look at the final result.

**TABLE 5-1**

Bob's Proposal—Scenario 1
Bob and Cindy's Asset List

| Item | Value | Net Value | Cindy | Bob |
|------|-------|-----------|-------|-----|
| *Home* | | | | |
| FMV | $220,000 | | | |
| Mortgage | 130,000 | | | |
| Equity | 90,000 | $ 90,000 | $ 90,000 | |
| *Rental property* | | | | |
| FMV | $ 90,000 | | | |
| Mortgage | 50,000 | | | |
| Selling costs | (6,300) | | | |
| Equity | 33,700 | 33,700 | 33,700 | |
| Business | | 200,000 | | $200,000 |
| IRAs | | 17,000 | 17,000 | |
| Debt | | (22,600) | (22,600) | |
| Total | | $318,100 | $118,100 | $200,000 |

Bob feels that since his business is so new it cannot be counted on, he is making a very generous proposal if he takes his business and gives Cindy *all* the other assets, as well as the debt.

Look at Table 5–2, Cindy's spreadsheet 1. The first column starts with the year 1996. The second column shows Cindy's age—she is now 32 years old. The next four columns—"Take-Home Pay," "Other Income," "Child Support," and "Maintenance Support"—are income columns as indicated by the head above them, "Income."

The column labeled "Take-Home Pay" has nothing in it for the first three years while Cindy completes her college degree. After finishing school, she expects to earn approximately $21,000 per year. The $17,000 shown in the fourth year is her *after-tax* take-home pay. The "4 percent" under "Take-Home Pay" indicates that it is increasing at 4 percent per year, the number also used for inflation in this case study. So, we are seeing that Cindy's income just keeps up with inflation. If inflation were 3 percent, we would show her income increasing at 3 percent.

The next column is labeled "Other Income." None is included since Cindy will not work for pay until she completes her degree. The

# Cindy's Spreadsheet (Scenario 1)

| | | Income | | | | Expenses | | | | Annual | Working | Fair Market Retirement | Value | Real Estate | Net |
|---|---|---|---|---|---|---|---|---|---|---|---|---|---|---|---|
| | | Take-Home Pay | Other Income | Child Support | Maint. Support | Living Expenses | Real Estate Payments | Other Expenses | Taxes on Maint. | Net Cash Flow | Capital | Accounts | Real Estate | Mortgage 15 | Worth |
| Year 1996 | Age 32 | 4.0% | 4.0% | 10 $6,000 | 1 $24,000 | 4.0% $48,241 | 15 $1,227 | | | | 5.5% $33,700 | 7.5% $17,000 | 4.0% $220,000 | 7.5% $130,000 | |
| 1996 | 32 | | | $6,000 | $24,000 | $33,514 | $14,722 | | $6,720 | ($24,961) | $10,592 | $18,275 | $228,800 | $125,023 | $132,645 |
| 1997 | 33 | | | 6,000 | 18,000 | 34,855 | 14,727 | | 2,700 | (28,282) | (5,261) | | 237,952 | 119,672 | 113,019 |
| 1998 | 34 | | | 6,000 | 18,000 | 36,249 | 14,727 | | 2,700 | (29,676) | (34,937) | | 247,470 | 113,920 | 98,613 |
| 1999 | 35 | $17,000 | | 6,000 | | 33,499 | 14,727 | ($4,200) | | (25,226) | (60,163) | | 257,369 | 107,737 | 89,469 |
| 2000 | 36 | 17,680 | | 6,000 | | 34,839 | 14,722 | | | (25,886) | (86,049) | | 267,664 | 101,090 | 80,525 |
| 2001 | 37 | 18,387 | | 6,000 | | 36,232 | 14,727 | | | (26,572) | (112,621) | | 278,370 | 93,944 | 71,805 |
| 2002 | 38 | 19,123 | | 6,000 | | 37,681 | 14,727 | | | (27,286) | (139,907) | | 289,505 | 86,263 | 63,335 |
| 2003 | 39 | 19,888 | | 6,000 | | 39,189 | 14,727 | | | (28,028) | (167,936) | | 301,085 | 78,005 | 55,144 |
| 2004 | 40 | 20,683 | | 6,000 | | 40,756 | 14,727 | | | (28,801) | (196,736) | | 313,129 | 69,128 | 47,264 |
| 2005 | 41 | 21,510 | | 6,000 | | 42,387 | 14,727 | | | (29,603) | (226,340) | | 325,654 | 59,585 | 39,729 |
| 2006 | 42 | 22,371 | | 3,000 | | 42,082 | 14,727 | (3,000) | | (30,438) | (256,778) | | 338,680 | 49,327 | 32,575 |
| 2007 | 43 | 23,266 | | 3,000 | | 43,765 | 14,727 | | | (31,227) | (288,005) | | 352,227 | 38,299 | 25,923 |
| 2008 | 44 | 24,196 | | 3,000 | | 45,516 | 14,727 | | | (32,047) | (320,052) | | 366,316 | 26,444 | 19,820 |
| 2009 | 45 | 25,164 | | 3,000 | | 43,472 | 14,727 | (3,865) | | (29,035) | (349,087) | | 380,060 | 13,700 | 18,182 |
| 2010 | 46 | 26,171 | | 3,000 | | 41,210 | 14,727 | (3,000) | | (29,767) | (378,854) | | 396,208 | (0) | 17,354 |
| 2011 | 47 | 27,218 | | | | 42,859 | | | | (15,641) | (394,495) | | 412,056 | | 17,561 |
| 2012 | 48 | 28,306 | | | | 44,573 | | | | (16,267) | (410,762) | | 428,538 | | 17,776 |
| 2013 | 49 | 29,438 | | | | 46,356 | | | | (16,918) | (427,680) | | 445,680 | | 18,000 |
| 2014 | 50 | 30,616 | | | | 48,210 | | | | (17,594) | (445,274) | | 463,507 | | 18,233 |
| 2015 | 51 | 31,841 | | | | 50,139 | | | | (18,298) | )(463,572) | | 482,047 | | 18,475 |
| 2016 | 52 | 33,114 | | | | 52,144 | | | | (19,030) | (482,602) | | 501,329 | | 18,727 |

Copyright 1987-1996 Quantum Financial, Inc.

next column, "Child Support," indicates she will receive $250 per month per child (or $6,000 per year) in child support for 10 years until the 9-year-old turns age 19. Then child support will decrease to $3,000 per year until the 5-year-old turns 19. This is based on Bob's offer.

The next column is "Maintenance Support." Bob offered $2,000 per month ($24,000) for one year and then $1,500 per month ($18,000) for two additional years.

The next four columns are under the head "Expenses." The first column under "Expenses" is "Living Expenses." The second one is labeled "Real Estate Payments." These two columns *together* equal Cindy's living expenses. They are separated into two columns so that the real estate payments column represents the principal and interest (P&I) payment *only*. It is not affected by inflation. The taxes and insurance part (T&I) of the house payment is reflected in the living expenses column. If the P&I were included in the living expenses column, that number—affected by inflation—would eventually become skewed. So the $48,241 above the line is her total yearly living expense, which is a combination of the two numbers below the line: $33,514 plus $14,727.

The "Other Expenses" column shows the changes in Cindy's living expenses. The first negative number—$4,200 in the fourth year—represents the fact that she has finished school and she no longer has school expenses of $350 per month ($4,200 per year). The second negative number—($3,000)—represents the year after the first child turns age 19 and leaves home. At that time, child support stops. Assume that Cindy no longer has the expenses associated with that child; therefore lower her living expenses by that amount. The third negative number—$3,865—represents the fact that she has paid off her debt. The fourth negative number reflects the fact that the second child has left home.

The column "Taxes on Maintenance" shows the taxes that she owes on her maintenance income. The next column, "Annual Net Cash Flow," shows whether there is positive or negative cash flow after netting the income columns with the expense columns. We see that Cindy has a negative $24,961 in the first year; in other words, her expenses are $24,961 more than her income.

The number from the "Annual Net Cash Flow" column is automatically subtracted from the next column, "Working Capital" (or added to if it is a positive number). Her working capital is shown earning an average of 5.5 percent after tax. Notice that Cindy's "Working Capital" column started out with $33,700, which was what remained after she sold the rental house. This asset was wiped out by the second year to help cover her negative cash flow.

The next column is labeled "Retirement Accounts." The assumption is that they will earn 7.5 percent before taxes. When the "Working Capital" column is depleted, the "Retirement Account" column will automatically cover the negative cash flow *less taxes and penalties* if Cindy is under 60. After 60, taxes are taken out. Notice that this depletes her "Retirement Account" column in the second year.

The next column, "Fair Market Value Real Estate," shows the value of Cindy's home. The 4 percent represents the average increase in real estate values in her part of her city over the past 10 years.

> By age 33, Cindy's spendable assets have been depleted. She does have the house—but she can't use the house to buy groceries.

The "Real Estate Mortgage" column shows the $130,000 mortgage on Cindy's home. The mortgage has 15 years remaining at 7.5 percent interest.

The final column, "Net Worth," is a combination of "Working Capital" plus the "Retirement Accounts" plus "Fair Market Value Real Estate" minus "Real Estate Mortgage." Figure 5–1 graphs net worth, which we'll consider later.

But first, let's look at Bob's spreadsheet—Table 5–3—to see how this scenario affects him financially. Bob's take-home pay ($57,570) is increasing at 4 percent per year, the same as Cindy's. The next column, "Living Expenses" shows his total annual living expenses—$24,600. The "Child Support" column shows the expense that he pays. The "Maintenance Support" column shows what it costs him in after-tax dollars to pay maintenance. The "Annual Net Cash Flow" column shows a positive $10,890 in the first year, which is added to the "Working Capital" column and is shown earning an average of 5.5 percent per year after taxes. The "Retirement Accounts" column shows that amount earning an average of 7.5 percent per year before taxes. The "Business" column shows the value of his business increasing at 4 percent per year. Bob's "Net Worth" column is a combination of "Working Capital" plus "Business."

Figure 5-1 graphs Bob and Cindy's net worth based on the previous assumptions. As you can see, the future doesn't appear too equitable. What changes can be made in scenario 1 to make this a more equitable settlement? The following changes represent scenario 2, which appears in spreadsheet form in Table 5–4.

**FIGURE 5-1**

Bob and Cindy's Scenario 1 Graph

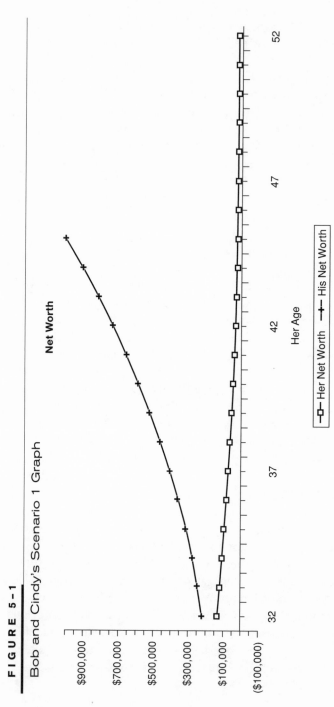

Net Worth

Copyright 1987–1996 Quantum Financial, Inc.

TABLE 5-3

## Bob's Spreadsheet (Scenario 1)

| Year 1996 | Age 33 | Income Take-Home Pay 4.0% $57,570 | Expenses Living Expenses 4.0% $24,600 | Other Expenses | Child Support | Maint. Support | Annual Net Cash Flow | Working Capital 5.5% | Retirement Accounts 7.5% | Business 4.0% $200,000 | Net Worth |
|---|---|---|---|---|---|---|---|---|---|---|---|
| 1996 | 33 | $57,570 | $24,600 | | $6,000 | $16,080 | $10,890 | $10,890 | | $208,000 | $218,890 |
| 1997 | 34 | 59,873 | 25,584 | | 6,000 | 12,060 | 16,229 | 27,718 | | 216,320 | 244,038 |
| 1998 | 35 | 62,268 | 26,607 | | 6,000 | 12,060 | 17,600 | 46,843 | | 224,973 | 271,815 |
| 1999 | 36 | 64,758 | 27,672 | | 6,000 | | 31,087 | 80,506 | | 233,972 | 314,477 |
| 2000 | 37 | 67,349 | 28,779 | | 6,000 | | 32,570 | 117,504 | | 243,331 | 360,834 |
| 2001 | 38 | 70,043 | 29,930 | | 6,000 | | 34,113 | 158,079 | | 253,064 | 411,143 |
| 2002 | 39 | 72,844 | 31,127 | | 6,000 | | 35,718 | 202,491 | | 263,186 | 465,678 |
| 2003 | 40 | 75,758 | 32,372 | | 6,000 | | 37,386 | 251,015 | | 273,714 | 524,729 |
| 2004 | 41 | 78,789 | 33,667 | | 6,000 | | 39,122 | 303,942 | | 284,662 | 588,605 |
| 2005 | 42 | 81,940 | 35,013 | | 6,000 | | 40,927 | 361,586 | | 296,049 | 657,635 |
| 2006 | 43 | 85,218 | 36,414 | | 3,000 | | 44,804 | 426,277 | | 307,891 | 734,167 |
| 2007 | 44 | 88,626 | 37,871 | | 3,000 | | 46,756 | 496,478 | | 320,206 | 816,684 |
| 2008 | 45 | 92,171 | 39,385 | | 3,000 | | 48,786 | 572,570 | | 333,015 | 905,585 |
| 2009 | 46 | 95,858 | 40,961 | | 3,000 | | 50,897 | 654,959 | | 346,335 | 1,001,294 |
| 2010 | 47 | 99,693 | 42,599 | | | | 57,093 | 748,075 | | 360,189 | 1,108,263 |
| 2011 | 48 | 103,680 | 44,303 | | | | 59,377 | 848,596 | | 374,596 | 1,223,192 |
| 2012 | 49 | 107,828 | 46,075 | | | | 61,752 | 957,021 | | 389,580 | 1,346,601 |
| 2013 | 50 | 112,141 | 47,918 | | | | 64,222 | 1,073,879 | | 405,163 | 1,479,043 |
| 2014 | 51 | 116,626 | 49,835 | | | | 66,791 | 1,199,734 | | 421,370 | 1,621,104 |
| 2015 | 52 | 121,291 | 51,828 | | | | 69,463 | 1,335,182 | | 438,225 | 1,773,407 |
| 2016 | 53 | 126,143 | 53,902 | | | | 72,241 | 1,480,858 | | 455,754 | 1,936,612 |

## TABLE 5–4

## Cindy's Spreadsheet (Scenario 2)

| | | Income | | | | Expenses | | | | Annual | Working | Retirement | Fair Market Value | Real Estate | Net |
|---|---|---|---|---|---|---|---|---|---|---|---|---|---|---|---|
| | | Take-Home Pay | Other Income | Child Support | Maint. Support | Living Expenses | Real Estate Payments | Other Expenses | Taxes on Maint. | Net Cash Flow | Capital | Accounts | Real Estate | Mortgage | Worth |
| | | 4.0% | | 10 | 1 | 4.0% | 15 | | | | 5.5% | 7.5% | 4.0% | 15 7.5% | |
| Year 1996 | 32 | | | $10,044 | $24,000 | $44,376 | $1,227 | | | | $33,700 | $17,000 | $220,000 | $130,000 | |
| 1996 | 32 | | | $10,044 | $24,000 | $29,649 | $14,727 | | $6,720 | ($17,052) | $ 18,501 | $18,275 | $228,800 | $125,023 | $140,554 |
| 1997 | 33 | | | 11,227 | 18,000 | 30,835 | 14,727 | | 2,700 | (19,035) | 483 | 19,646 | 237,952 | 119,672 | 138,409 |
| 1998 | 34 | | | 11,227 | 18,000 | 32,068 | 14,727 | | 2,700 | (20,269) | (7,024) | | 247,470 | 113,920 | 126,526 |
| 1999 | 35 | $17,000 | $5,866 | 14,772 | | 29,151 | 14,727 | ($4,200) | | (6,240) | (13,264) | | 257,369 | 107,737 | 136,368 |
| 2000 | 36 | 17,680 | 5,866 | 14,772 | | 30,317 | 14,727 | | | (6,726) | (19,991) | | 267,664 | 101,090 | 146,583 |
| 2001 | 37 | 18,387 | 5,866 | 14,772 | | 31,530 | 14,727 | | | (7,232) | (27,223) | | 278,370 | 93,944 | 157,203 |
| 2002 | 38 | 19,123 | 5,866 | 14,772 | | 32,791 | 14,727 | | | (7,758) | (34,980) | | 289.50 | 86,263 | 168,262 |
| 2003 | 39 | 19,888 | 5,866 | 14,772 | | 34,103 | 14,727 | | | (8,304) | (43,285) | | 301,08 | 78,005 | 179,795 |
| 2004 | 40 | 20,683 | | 14,772 | | 35,467 | 14,727 | | | (14,739) | (58,024) | | 313,129 | 69,128 | 185,977 |
| 2005 | 41 | 21,510 | | 14,772 | | 36,885 | 14,727 | | | (15,330) | (73,354) | | 325,654 | 59,585 | 192,714 |
| 2006 | 42 | 22,371 | | 9,516 | | 33,105 | 14,727 | (5,256) | | (15,945) | (89,300) | | 338,680 | 49,327 | 200,054 |
| 2007 | 43 | 23,266 | | 9,516 | | 34,429 | 14,727 | | | (16,375) | (105,674) | | 352,227 | 38,299 | 208,254 |
| 2008 | 44 | 24,196 | | 9,516 | | 35,806 | 14,727 | | | (16,821) | (122,496) | | 366,316 | 26,444 | 217,377 |
| 2009 | 45 | 25,164 | | 9,516 | | 37,238 | 14,727 | | | (17,286) | (139,781) | | 380,060 | 13,700 | 227,488 |
| 2010 | 46 | 26,171 | | | | 29,212 | 14,727 | (9,516) | | (17,769) | (157,550) | | 396,208 | (0) | 238,658 |
| 2011 | 47 | 27,218 | | | | 30,380 | | | | (3,163) | (160,713) | | 412,056 | | 251,343 |
| 2012 | 48 | 28,306 | | | | 31,596 | | | | (3,289) | (164,002) | | 428,538 | | 264,536 |
| 2013 | 49 | 29,438 | | | | 32,860 | | | | (3,421) | (167,423) | | 445,680 | | 278,256 |
| 2014 | 50 | 30,616 | | | | 34,174 | | | | (3,558) | (170,981) | | 463,507 | | 292,526 |
| 2015 | 51 | 31,841 | | | | 35,541 | | | | (3,700) | (174,681) | | 482,047 | | 307,366 |
| 2016 | 52 | 33,114 | | | | 36,962 | | | | (3,848) | (178,529) | | 501,329 | | 322,800 |

Copyright 1987–1996 Quantum Financial, Inc.

1. Cindy will receive proper child support according to the child support guidelines—$837 per month ($10,044 per year) until the first child is 19 years old, at which time it decreases. Notice that the amount of child support is affected by the amount of maintenance paid to her and her earnings.

2. Bob will assume the debt of $22,600. Note that (1) his expenses are increased in scenario 2 to include his making debt payments and (2) Cindy's expenses are decreased.

3. A property settlement note of $18,350 is paid to Cindy starting in the fourth year at which time the payments are $5,866 per year for five years (assuming 7 percent interest). This is shown in the "Other Income" column.

How does scenario 2 affect Bob? Look at Table 5–5, Bob's revised spreadsheet. The changes are in the amount he is paying in child support and the property settlement note shown in the column to the right of "Maintenance Support." He still has positive cash flow.

Figure 5–2 graphs all the data of scenario 2. Notice that scenario 2 helps Cindy some but not enough. The problem is that she is too emotionally tied to an asset (the house) that she cannot afford. Her house payments of $1,500 per month, combined with no earned income for three years, create a disaster for her.

Let's see what happens if we come up with scenario 3, where she sells the house in the first year after divorce, keeps the property settlement note the same, and extends the $1,500 per month maintenance for an additional three years. Table 5–6 details the changes. Notice that her take-home pay is still the same. She is still going to school for three years before bringing home $17,000 per year. The "Other Income" column reflects the property settlement note. Child support is according to the child support guidelines. The "Maintenance Support" column shows maintenance of $2,000 per month ($24,000 for one year) and then $1,500 per month ($18,000 per year) for five years.

In scenario 3, Cindy's living expenses and real estate payments are the same as in scenario 2 for the first year. Then, in the next year, assume that the house has been sold and that Cindy rents an apartment for $780 per month. The taxes and insurance on the house

After the first year, her "Annual Net Cash Flow" column has much lower negatives than before. In fact, she then has positive cash flow for years three through six.

# TABLE 5-5

## Bob's Spreadsheet (Scenario 2)

| Year | Age | Income Take-Home Pay 4.0% $57,570 | Living Expenses 4.0% $28,465 | Other Expenses | Child Support | Maint. Support | Annual Net Cash Flow | Working Capital 5.5% | Retirement Accounts 7.5% | Business 4.0% $200,000 | Net Worth |
|---|---|---|---|---|---|---|---|---|---|---|---|
| 1996 | 33 | $57,570 | $28,465 | | $10,044 | $16,080 | $ 2,981 | $ 2,981 | | $208.000 | $210.981 |
| 1997 | 34 | 59,873 | 29,604 | | 11,227 | 12,060 | 6,982 | 10,127 | | 216,320 | 226,447 |
| 1998 | 35 | 62,268 | 30,788 | | 11,227 | 12,060 | 8,193 | 18,877 | | 224,973 | 243,850 |
| 1999 | 36 | 64,758 | 32,019 | | 14,772 | | 17,967 | 37,883 | | 233,972 | 271,854 |
| 2000 | 37 | 67,349 | 33,300 | | 14,772 | | 19,277 | 59,243 | | 243,331 | 302,573 |
| 2001 | 38 | 70,043 | 34,632 | | 14,772 | | 20,639 | 83,140 | | 253,064 | 336,204 |
| 2002 | 39 | 72,844 | 36,017 | | 14,772 | | 22,055 | 109,768 | | 263,186 | 372,954 |
| 2003 | 40 | 75,758 | 37,458 | | 14,772 | | 23,528 | 139,333 | | 273,714 | 413,047 |
| 2004 | 41 | 78,789 | 38,956 | | 14,772 | | 25,060 | 172,057 | | 284,662 | 456,719 |
| 2005 | 42 | 81,940 | 40,515 | | 14,772 | | 26,653 | 208,173 | | 296,049 | 504,222 |
| 2006 | 43 | 85,218 | 42,135 | | 9,516 | | 33,567 | 253,189 | | 307,891 | 561,080 |
| 2007 | 44 | 88,626 | 43,821 | | 9,516 | | 35,290 | 302,404 | | 320,206 | 622,611 |
| 2008 | 45 | 92,171 | 45,573 | | 9,516 | | 37,082 | 356,119 | | 333,015 | 689,133 |
| 2009 | 46 | 95,858 | 43,531 | ($3,865) | 9,516 | | 42,811 | 418,516 | | 346,335 | 764,851 |
| 2010 | 47 | 99,693 | 45,273 | | | | 54,420 | 495,955 | | 360,189 | 856,143 |
| 2011 | 48 | 103,680 | 47,083 | | | | 56,597 | 579,829 | | 374,596 | 954,425 |
| 2012 | 49 | 107,828 | 48,967 | | | | 58,861 | 670,580 | | 389,580 | 1,060,160 |
| 2013 | 50 | 112,141 | 50,025 | | | | 61,215 | 768,677 | | 405,163 | 1,173,841 |
| 2014 | 51 | 116,626 | 52,963 | | | | 63,664 | 874,618 | | 421,370 | 1,295,988 |
| 2015 | 52 | 121,291 | 55,081 | | | | 66,210 | 988,933 | | 438,225 | 1,427,157 |
| 2016 | 53 | 126,143 | 57,284 | | | | 68,859 | 1,112,183 | | 455,754 | 1,576,936 |

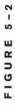

## F I G U R E  5 – 2

### Bob and Cindy's Scenario 2 Graph

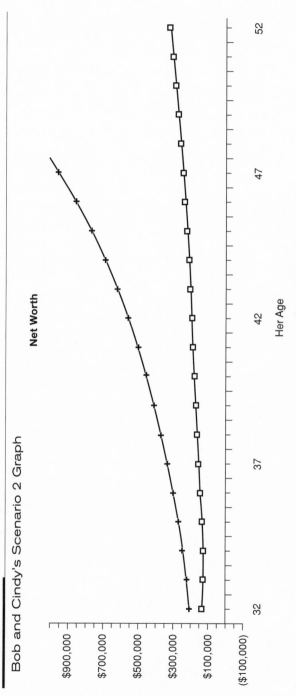

**Net Worth**

Her Age

—□— Her Net Worth   —+— His Net Worth

Copyright 1987–1996 Quantum Financial, Inc.

# TABLE 5 - 6

## Cindy's Spreadsheet (Scenario 3)

| | | Income | | | | Expenses | | | | Annual | Working | Retirement | Fair Market Value | Real Estate | Net |
|---|---|---|---|---|---|---|---|---|---|---|---|---|---|---|---|
| | | Take-Home Pay | Other Income | Child Support | Maint. Support | Living Expenses | Real Estate Payments | Other Expenses | Taxes on Maint. | Net Cash Flow | Capital | Accounts | Real Estate | Mortgage | Worth |
| | | 4.0% | | 10 | 1 | 4.0% | 1 | | | | 5.5% | 7.5% | 4.0% | 15 7.5% | |
| Year 1996 | 32 | | | $10,044 | $24,000 | $29,649 | $1,227 | | | | $33,700 | $17,000 | $220,000 | $130,000 | |
| 1996 | 32 | | | $10,044 | $24,000 | $29,649 | $14,727 | | $6,720 | ($17,052) | $ 18,501 | $18,275 | $228,800 | $125,023 | $140,554 |
| 1997 | 33 | | | 11,227 | 18,000 | 37,507 | | | 2,700 | (10,980) | 95,597 | 19,646 | | | 115,243 |
| 1998 | 34 | | | 11,227 | 18,000 | 39,007 | | | 2,700 | (12,480) | 88,375 | 21,119 | | | 109,494 |
| 1999 | 35 | $17,000 | $5,866 | 10,168 | 18,000 | 36,368 | | ($4,200) | 5,040 | 9,626 | 102,862 | 22,703 | | | 125,565 |
| 2000 | 36 | 17,680 | 5,866 | 10,168 | 18,000 | 37,822 | | | 5,040 | 8,852 | 117,371 | 24,406 | | | 141,776 |
| 2001 | 37 | 18,387 | 5,866 | 10,168 | 18,000 | 39,335 | | | 5,040 | 8,046 | 131,872 | 26,236 | | | 158,108 |
| 2002 | 38 | 19,123 | 5,866 | 14,772 | | 40,909 | | | | (1,148) | 137,977 | 28,204 | | | 166,181 |
| 2003 | 39 | 19,888 | 5,866 | 14,772 | | 42,545 | | | | (2,019) | 143,547 | 30,319 | | | 173,866 |
| 2004 | 40 | 20,683 | | 14,772 | | 44,247 | | | | (8,792) | 142,650 | 32,593 | | | 175,243 |
| 2005 | 41 | 21,510 | | 14,772 | | 46,017 | | | | (9,734) | 140,762 | 35,038 | | | 175,799 |
| 2006 | 42 | 22,371 | | 9,516 | | 42,601 | | (5,256) | | (10,714) | 137,789 | 37,665 | | | 175,455 |
| 2007 | 43 | 23,266 | | 9,516 | | 44,305 | | | | (11,524) | 133,844 | 40,490 | | | 174,334 |
| 2008 | 44 | 24,196 | | 9,516 | | 46,078 | | | | (12,365) | 128,840 | 43,527 | | | 172,367 |
| 2009 | 45 | 25,164 | | 9,516 | | 47,921 | | | | (13,240) | 122,686 | 46,792 | | | 169,477 |
| 2010 | 46 | 26,171 | | | | 40,321 | | (9,516) | | (14,151) | 115,283 | 50,301 | | | 165,584 |
| 2011 | 47 | 27,218 | | | | 41,934 | | | | (14,717) | 106,907 | 54,073 | | | 160,980 |
| 2012 | 48 | 28,306 | | | | 43,612 | | | | (15,305) | 97,481 | 58,129 | | | 155,610 |
| 2013 | 49 | 29,438 | | | | 45,356 | | | | (15,918) | 86,925 | 62,489 | | | 149,414 |
| 2014 | 50 | 30,616 | | | | 47,170 | | | | (16,554) | 75,152 | 67,175 | | | 142,327 |
| 2015 | 51 | 31,841 | | | | 49,057 | | | | (17,217) | 62,068 | 72,213 | | | 134,282 |
| 2016 | 52 | 33,114 | | | | 51,019 | | | | (17,905) | 47,577 | 77,629 | | | 125,207 |

66

($224 per month) had been included in the "Living Expenses" column in past scenarios. In scenario 3 her net increase in the "Living Expenses" column is $556 per month ($6,672 per year).

When the house is sold and the selling costs and mortgage balance are deducted from the profits, the remaining balance is added to the "Working Capital" column in the second year. With these adjustments, she still has working capital at age 52.

In Table 5–7, we find that Bob still has positive cash flow and his assets continue to increase in value. Figure 5–3 graphs all Bob's data in scenario 3.

In scenario 4, assume that Cindy did not sell the rental house but moved into it instead, and maintenance is $2,500 per month for one year, $2,000 per month for two years, and $1,500 per month for three years. Table 5–8 presents this data.

First of all, look at the "Fair Market Value Real Estate" column. Notice that in the second year, the value of her house is $90,000 and the real estate mortgage is $50,000. This shows that she is now living in the rental house.

The "Real Estate Payments" column shows the reduction in the monthly payment.

Cindy no longer has the $33,700 profit from selling the rental to invest in her "Working Capital" column. But the proceeds from selling the house help her out. The "Working Capital" column shows that her proceeds will last for a much longer time if she is careful with her spending.

Table 5–9 shows how scenario 4 affects Bob. The higher maintenance takes essentially all his cash flow in the first year. When maintenance reduces in the second year, his annual net cash flow increases and continues to increase. The results are shown in Figure 5–4.

It doesn't make economic sense for Cindy to keep a house with a $1,500 per month house payment when she has no income and she is relying on maintenance to make that payment for her. She could rent a house in that area for $800 to 900 per month. Maintenance cannot be counted on. This is a case that will take a lot of counseling on cash flow and budgeting. Both parties must understand that whatever scenario is followed will have major impacts on their finances, emotions, parenting, and relationship.

# TABLE 5-7

## Bob's Spreadsheet (Scenario 3)

| Year 1996 | Age 33 | Income Take-Home Pay 4.0% $57,570 | Expenses Living Expenses 4.0% $28,465 | Other Expenses | Child Support | Maint. Support | Annual Net Cash Flow | Working Capital 5.5% | Retirement Accounts 7.5% | Business 4.0% $200,000 | Net Worth |
|---|---|---|---|---|---|---|---|---|---|---|---|
| 1996 | 33 | $ 57,570 | $28,465 | | $10,044 | $16,080 | $ 2,981 | $ 2,981 | | $208,000 | $ 210,981 |
| 1997 | 34 | 59,873 | 29,604 | | 11,227 | 12,060 | 6,982 | 10,127 | | 216,320 | 226,447 |
| 1998 | 35 | 62,268 | 30,788 | | 11,227 | 12,060 | 8,193 | 18,877 | | 224,973 | 243,850 |
| 1999 | 36 | 64,758 | 32,019 | | 10,168 | 12,060 | 10,511 | 30,427 | | 233,972 | 264,398 |
| 2000 | 37 | 67,349 | 33,300 | | 10,168 | 12,060 | 11,821 | 43,921 | | 243,331 | 287,251 |
| 2001 | 38 | 70,043 | 34,632 | | 10,168 | 12,060 | 13,183 | 59,519 | | 253,064 | 312,583 |
| 2002 | 39 | 72,844 | 36,017 | | 14,772 | | 22,055 | 84,848 | | 263,186 | 348,034 |
| 2003 | 40 | 75,758 | 37,458 | | 14,772 | | 23,528 | 113,043 | | 273,714 | 386,756 |
| 2004 | 41 | 78,789 | 38,956 | | 14,772 | | 25,060 | 144,320 | | 284,662 | 428,982 |
| 2005 | 42 | 81,940 | 40,515 | | 14,772 | | 26,653 | 178,911 | | 296,049 | 474,960 |
| 2006 | 43 | 85,218 | 42,135 | | 9,516 | | 33,567 | 222,318 | | 307,891 | 530,209 |
| 2007 | 44 | 88,626 | 43,821 | | 9,516 | | 35,290 | 269,835 | | 320,206 | 590,042 |
| 2008 | 45 | 92,171 | 45,573 | | 9,516 | | 37,082 | 321,758 | | 333,015 | 654,773 |
| 2009 | 46 | 95,858 | 43,531 | ($3,865) | 9,516 | | 42,811 | 418,516 | | 346,335 | 728,601 |
| 2010 | 47 | 99,693 | 45,273 | | | | 54,420 | 457,710 | | 360,189 | 817,899 |
| 2011 | 48 | 103,680 | 47,083 | | | | 56,597 | 539,481 | | 374,596 | 914,078 |
| 2012 | 49 | 107,828 | 48,967 | | | | 58,861 | 628,013 | | 389,580 | 1,017,594 |
| 2013 | 50 | 112,141 | 50,925 | | | | 61,215 | 723,769 | | 405,163 | 1,128,933 |
| 2014 | 51 | 116,626 | 52,963 | | | | 63,664 | 827,240 | | 421,370 | 1,248,610 |
| 2015 | 52 | 121,291 | 55,081 | | | | 66,210 | 938,949 | | 438,225 | 1,377,174 |
| 2016 | 53 | 126,143 | 57,284 | | | | 68,859 | 1,059,450 | | 455,754 | 1,515,203 |

Copyright 1987–1996 Quantum Financial, Inc.

**FIGURE 5 – 3**

Bob and Cindy's Scenario 3 Graph

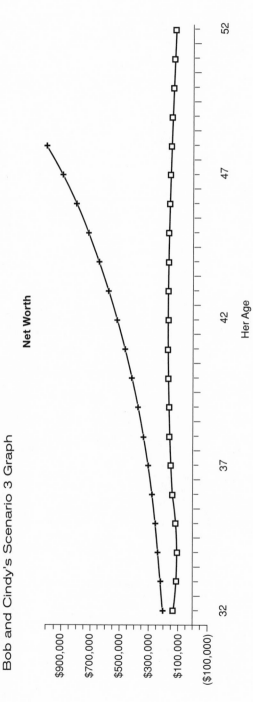

**Net Worth**

**TABLE 5-8**

## Cindy's Spreadsheet (Scenario 4)

| | | Income | | | | Expenses | | | | Annual | Working | Retirement | Fair Market Value | Real Estate | Net |
|---|---|---|---|---|---|---|---|---|---|---|---|---|---|---|---|
| | | Take-Home Pay 4.0% | Other Income | Child Support 10 | Maint. Support 1 | Living Expenses 4.0% | Real Estate Payments 12 | Other Expenses | Taxes on Maint. | Net Cash Flow | Capital 5.5% | Accounts 7.5% | Real Estate 4.0% | Mortgage 15 7.5% | Worth |
| Year 1996 | Age 32 | | | $8,863 | $30,000 | $29,649 | $1,227 | | | | | $17,000 | $220,000 | $130,000 | |
| 1996 | 32 | | | $8,863 | $30,000 | $29,649 | $14,727 | | $8,400 | ($13,913) | (2,894) | | $228,800 | $125,023 | $100,884 |
| 1997 | 33 | | | 10,044 | 24,000 | 30,835 | 7,200 | | 7,200 | (11,191) | 74,410 | | 90,000 | 50,000 | 114,410 |
| 1998 | 34 | | | 10,044 | 24,000 | 32,068 | 7,200 | | 6,720 | (11,944) | 66,558 | | 93,600 | 46,550 | 113,608 |
| 1999 | 35 | $17,000 | $5,866 | 10,168 | 18,000 | 29,151 | 7,200 | ($4,200) | 5,040 | 9,643 | 79,862 | | 97,344 | 42,841 | 134,364 |
| 2000 | 36 | 17,680 | 5,866 | 10,168 | 18,000 | 30,317 | 7,200 | | 5,040 | 9,157 | 93,411 | | 101,238 | 38,854 | 155,794 |
| 2001 | 37 | 18,387 | 5,866 | 10,168 | 18,000 | 31,530 | 7,200 | | 5,040 | 8,651 | 107,200 | | 105,287 | 34,568 | 177,919 |
| 2002 | 38 | 19,123 | 5,866 | 14,772 | | 32,791 | 7,200 | | | (230) | 112,865 | | 109,499 | 29,961 | 192,403 |
| 2003 | 39 | 19,888 | 5,866 | 14,772 | | 34,103 | 7,200 | | | (777) | 118,296 | | 113,879 | 25,008 | 207,167 |
| 2004 | 40 | 20,683 | | 14,772 | | 35,467 | 7,200 | | | (7,212) | 117,591 | | 118,434 | 19,684 | 216,341 |
| 2005 | 41 | 21,510 | | 14,772 | | 36,885 | 7,200 | | | (7,803) | 116,255 | | 123,171 | 13,960 | 225,466 |
| 2006 | 42 | 22,371 | | 9,516 | | 33,105 | 7,200 | (5,256) | | (8,418) | 114,231 | | 128,098 | 7,807 | 234,522 |
| 2007 | 43 | 23,266 | | 9,516 | | 34,429 | 7,200 | | | (8,847) | 111,666 | | 133,222 | 1,193 | 243,696 |
| 2008 | 44 | 24,196 | | 9,516 | | 35,806 | | | | (2,094) | 115,714 | | 138,551 | | 254,265 |
| 2009 | 45 | 25,164 | | 9,516 | | 37,239 | | | | (2,558) | 119,520 | | 144,093 | | 263,613 |
| 2010 | 46 | 26,171 | | | | 29,212 | | (9,516) | | (3,041) | 123,052 | | 149,857 | | 272,909 |
| 2011 | 47 | 27,218 | | | | 30,381 | | | | (3,163) | 126,657 | | 155,851 | | 282,508 |
| 2012 | 48 | 28,306 | | | | 31,596 | | | | (3,290) | 130,333 | | 162,085 | | 292,418 |
| 2013 | 49 | 29,438 | | | | 32,860 | | | | (3,421) | 134,081 | | 168,568 | | 302,649 |
| 2014 | 50 | 30,616 | | | | 34,174 | | | | (3,558) | 137,897 | | 175,311 | | 313,208 |
| 2015 | 51 | 31,841 | | | | 35,541 | | | | (3,700) | 141,781 | | 182,323 | | 324,105 |
| 2016 | 52 | 33,114 | | | | 36,963 | | | | (3,848) | 145,731 | | 189,616 | | 335,347 |

# TABLE 5-9

## Bob's Spreadsheet (Scenario 4)

| Year | Age | Income Take-Home Pay 4.0% $57,570 | Expenses Living Expenses 4.0% $28,465 | Other Expenses | Child Support | Maint. Support | Annual Net Cash Flow | Working Capital 5.5% | Retirement Accounts 7.5% | Business 4.0% $200,000 | Net Worth |
|------|-----|------|------|------|------|------|------|------|------|------|------|
| 1996 | 33 | $ 57,570 | $28,465 | | $8,863 | $20,100 | $ 142 | $ 142 | | $208,000 | $208,142 |
| 1997 | 34 | 59,873 | 29,604 | | 10,044 | 16,080 | 4,145 | 4,295 | | 216,320 | 220,615 |
| 1998 | 35 | 62,268 | 30,788 | | 10,044 | 16,080 | 5,356 | 9,887 | | 224,973 | 234,860 |
| 1999 | 36 | 64,758 | 32,019 | | 10,168 | 12,060 | 10,511 | 20,942 | | 233,972 | 254,914 |
| 2000 | 37 | 67,349 | 33,300 | | 10,168 | 12,060 | 11,821 | 33,915 | | 243,331 | 277,245 |
| 2001 | 38 | 70,043 | 34,632 | | 10,168 | 12,060 | 13,183 | 48,963 | | 253,064 | 302,027 |
| 2002 | 39 | 72,844 | 36,017 | | 14,772 | | 22,055 | 73,711 | | 263,186 | 336,897 |
| 2003 | 40 | 75,758 | 37,458 | | 14,772 | | 23,528 | 101,293 | | 273,714 | 375,007 |
| 2004 | 41 | 78,789 | 38,956 | | 14,772 | | 25,060 | 131,924 | | 284,662 | 416,587 |
| 2005 | 42 | 81,940 | 40,515 | | 14,772 | | 26,653 | 165,834 | | 296,049 | 461,883 |
| 2006 | 43 | 85,218 | 42,135 | | 9,516 | | 33,567 | 208,521 | | 307,891 | 516,412 |
| 2007 | 44 | 88,626 | 43,821 | | 9,516 | | 35,290 | 255,280 | | 320,206 | 575,486 |
| 2008 | 45 | 92,171 | 45,573 | ($3,865) | 9,516 | | 37,082 | 306,402 | | 333,015 | 639,417 |
| 2009 | 46 | 95,858 | 43,531 | | 9,516 | | 42,811 | 366,065 | | 346,335 | 712,400 |
| 2010 | 47 | 99,693 | 45,273 | | | | 54,420 | 440,619 | | 360,189 | 800,807 |
| 2011 | 48 | 103,680 | 47,083 | | | | 56,597 | 521,450 | | 374,596 | 896,046 |
| 2012 | 49 | 107,828 | 48,967 | | | | 58,861 | 608,990 | | 389,580 | 998,570 |
| 2013 | 50 | 112,141 | 50,925 | | | | 61,215 | 703,700 | | 405,163 | 1,108,863 |
| 2014 | 51 | 116,626 | 52,963 | | | | 63,664 | 806,067 | | 421,370 | 1,227,437 |
| 2015 | 52 | 121,291 | 55,081 | | | | 66,210 | 916,611 | | 438,225 | 1,354,835 |
| 2016 | 53 | 126,143 | 57,284 | | | | 68,859 | 1,035,883 | | 455,754 | 1,491,637 |

72

**FIGURE 5 - 4**

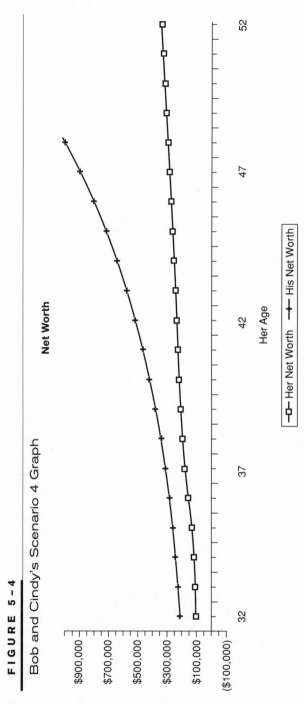

Bob and Cindy's Scenario 4 Graph

Net Worth

Her Age

—□— Her Net Worth  —+— His Net Worth

$900,000
$700,000
$500,000
$300,000
$100,000
($100,000)

32    37    42    47    52

## CHAPTER 6

# Pensions–His, Hers, . . . or Theirs

This chapter is not meant to make you an expert on pensions, nor can it teach you how to evaluate pensions. There are volumes written on this subject! Rather, it is to make you aware of pensions' variations and the challenges they present to your client's fair settlement.

Pensions (also referred to as retirement plans) are recognized as part of the joint property acquired during the marriage and as part of the assets to be divided upon divorce. Pension and retirement benefits earned during the marriage are potentially of great value. In a long marriage, they may be the couple's most valuable asset.

## METHODS OF DIVIDING A PENSION

The courts are struggling with the problem of how to value and divide pensions. For some cases, they must value the interest in a retirement plan. This interest will not include any portion acquired either after the divorce or, in most states, before the marriage. To figure out how much of the pension is marital property, you need to know the specifics of the employee's retirement plan.

There are two main schools of thought when it comes to dividing pension benefits. The first is the *buyout* or *cashout method,* which awards the nonemployee spouse a lump sum settlement—or a marital asset of equal value—at the time of divorce in return for the employee's keeping the pension.

The second method is the *deferred division* or *future share method* where no present value is determined. Each spouse is awarded a share of the benefits if and when they are paid.

In a defined-contribution plan, there is very little problem identifying the value of the account. Monthly or quarterly statements show the dollar amount available to be divided in either the buyout method or future share method.

There is a bewildering array of basic plans with countless diverse provisions. Anyone who has tried to explain retirement plans and pensions knows that it is often very confusing. There are two main types of retirement or pension plans: defined-contribution and defined-benefit. Here's a basic explanation of the two types and how they work. This information is important when presenting the different options to clients.

## DEFINED-CONTRIBUTION PLANS

One type of defined-contribution retirement plan is the 401(k). But even in the overall group of 401(k)s, there are different types with different rules. Each company can set its own rules for its retirement plans as long as the plan is approved by the IRS.

## Three Types of Defined Contribution Plans

Defined contribution plans differ depending on who contributes the money to the plan. It can be the employee, the employer, or a combination of the two. Here's an explanation of how defined contribution works.

Let's say there are three employees. Employee A is married and works for a company that has a 401(k). He puts all of his retirement money into the 401(k) and the company does not match any of his funds. He has worked there for three years and he has accumulated $1,500 in his plan. Any money that an employee puts into a 401(k) is the employee's—he or she is 100 percent vested. If he quits or is fired, he can take all of this money with him. He can use it as income, declaring such to the IRS (and, most likely, receiving a penalty of 10 percent of the withdrawn amount) or he can roll it over to an IRA. At the end of three years, employee A and his wife are getting a divorce.

|                                  | **Employee A** |
|----------------------------------|----------------|
| Length of employment             | 3 years        |
| 401(k) value at time of divorce  | $1,500         |
| Percent vested                   | 100%           |
| Marital portion                  | $1,500         |

Employee B works for a company where only the employer contributes money to the 401(k). The employee does not put anything in. He has worked there for three years and his 401(k) is worth $1,500. The company uses a vesting schedule, which regulates how much money he can take with him if he quits or is fired. The amount depends on how long he has worked for the company. A typical vesting schedule has an employee 20 percent vested in three years, 60 percent vested in five years, and 100 percent vested in seven years. Employee B is 30 percent vested. Therefore, his 401(k) today is worth 30 percent of $1,500 (i.e., $450). The lower amount, $450, is assigned to the marital pot of assets.

|  | Employee A | Employee B |
| --- | --- | --- |
| Length of employment | 3 years | 3 years |
| Value at time of divorce | $1,500 | $1,500 |
| Percent vested | 100% | 30% |
| Marital portion | $1,500 | $450 |

Employee C works for a company whose policy is that every dollar he puts in the 401(k) is matched with 50 cents. He has worked there for three years and he has $1,500 in his 401(k). Of this $1,500, he has put in $1,000 and the company has put in $500 with its matching program. He is 30 percent vested. However, the $1,000 that he put in was his money, so he is 100 percent vested in that amount and he can take that whole $1,000. He can also take 30 percent of the $500 (i.e., $150). Employee C's marital portion of this 401(k) is worth $1,150.

|  | Employee A | Employee B | Employee C |
| --- | --- | --- | --- |
| Employee/employer contribution |  |  | $1/50 cents |
| Length of employment | 3 years | 3 years | 3 years |
| Value at time of divorce | $1,500 | $1,500 | $1,500 |
| Percent vested | 100% | 30% | 30% |
| Marital portion | $1,500 | $450 | $1,000/$500 |
|  |  |  | $1,000 |
|  |  |  | $ 150 |
|  |  |  | $1,150 |

You have three different defined contribution plans valued three different ways, depending on the company's policy. To divide this asset in a divorce, a QDRO (qualified domestic relations order) is used.

## Qualified Domestic Relations Order (QDRO)

A 1986 amendment to the Retirement Equity Act gives state courts the power to order the division of certain pension and retirement plans. The plans covered under this federal law are public employers that are covered by the Employee Retirement Income Security Act of 1974 (ERISA).

The QDRO is an order from the court to the retirement plan administrator spelling out how the plan's benefits are to be assigned to each party in a divorce. It is a legal document, creating both problems and liabilities with it. QDROs must be done by professionals who know what they are doing—an attorney or someone who specializes in QDROs. *Warning: A financial planner should probably never be involved with drafting a QDRO.*

Plans divisible by a QDRO include defined-contribution plans, defined-benefit plans, 401(k)s, thrift savings plans, some profit-sharing and money-purchase plans, Keogh plans, tax-sheltered annuities, Employee Stock Ownership Plan (ESOPs), and the old Payroll Based Employee Stock Ownership Plan (PAYSOPs). Plans that are not divisible by a QDRO include some plans of small employers not covered by ERISA as well as many public employee group funds such as funds of police and fire groups, and city, state, and other governmental employees including federal employees.

**The terms of the QDRO state how the pension is to be to divided between the parties.**

The QDRO is sent to the employer's pension plan administrator. It tells how much of the money in the plan is to be sent to the spouse of the employee. This amount can range from zero to 100 percent, depending on how they have divided the other assets. It does not automatically mean 50 percent. A phrase often used by attorneys is, "We are going to QDRO that pension," and they are usually thinking about a 50 percent split because that is most typical. By definition, however, it does not mean 50 percent. Typically, the QDRO tells not only how the money in the plan is to be divided, but what is to happen to the money when the parties die.

## Transferring Assets from a Defined-Contribution Plan

What happens when the exspouse receives the 401(k) asset? For instance, Esther was married to an airline pilot who was nearing retirement. They were both age 55. There was $640,000 in his 401(k) and the retirement plan was prepared to transfer $320,000 to her IRA. She could transfer the money to an IRA and pay no taxes on this amount until she withdraws funds from the IRA. But Esther's attorney's fees were $60,000 and she needed another $20,000 to fix her roof. She said, "I need $80,000." She held back $80,000 of the monies before transferring the remaining $240,000 into her IRA. She was able to spend the $80,000.

There are some specific rules to be aware of. One IRS rule says that any money received from a qualified plan in a divorce situation only can be spent without penalty even if the recipient is under age 59 ½. Esther did have to pay the taxes on the entire amount because she had to declare the $80,000 as income, but she did not have to pay the 10 percent early withdrawal penalty.

Normally, distributions made before the participant attains age 59 ½ are called *early distributions,* and are subject to a 10 percent penalty tax. The tax does not apply to early distributions upon death or disability, annuity payments for the life expectancy of the individual, or distributions made to an exspouse by a QDRO.

Tax Code section (72)(t)(2)(D) says that when you take money out of a *qualified* plan in accordance with a written divorce instrument (a QDRO), the recipient can spend any or all of it without paying the 10 percent penalty.

After the money from a pension plan goes into an IRA, which is not considered a qualified plan, Esther is held to the early withdrawal rule. If she says, "Oh I forgot. I need another $5,000 to buy a car," it is too late. She will have to pay the 10 percent penalty and the taxes on that money.

You must understand the difference between *rolling over* money from a qualified plan and *transferring money* from a qualified plan. The Unemployment Compensation Amendment Act (UCA), which took effect in January 1993, states that any monies taken out of a qualified plan or tax-sheltered annuity are subject to 20 percent withholding. This rule does not apply to IRAs or SEPs.

For example, Henry was to receive his ex-wife Ginny's 401(k) of $100,000, which was invested in the ABC Mutual Fund. He asked the ABC Fund to send him the money so he could do a rollover of the money into a different mutual fund of his choice. The ABC Fund sent Henry $80,000—the amount remaining after it took out the 20 percent withholding tax. Henry deposited the $80,000 in his new IRA mutual fund. He could have added the $20,000 withheld for taxes, but he didn't have $20,000 to spare even though the IRS would have refunded that amount to him after he filed his taxes.

Since he could not come up with the $20,000, the next April when he filed his tax return, he paid an extra $6,600 in state and federal taxes plus $2,000 for the 10 percent penalty for *premature distribution!* Of course, when he eventually takes his IRA money, $20,000 in taxes will already have been paid. If Henry had instead *transferred* the $100,000 from the ABC Mutual Fund to his new fund, he would have $100,000 in his new fund (instead of $80,000) and would have saved $8,600 in taxes and penalties. Remember the effect of having an extra $20,000 growing tax-free!.

To *transfer funds,* Henry could have instructed the ABC Mutual Fund to send his $100,000 directly to the new IRA account he had just set up with his new mutual fund.

If a QDRO is used to order a lump sum to be paid to a former spouse from a defined-contribution plan, be sure to notify the plan administrator whether the funds are to be transferred in whole or in

> IRA transfers must be made directly between trustees and not by a rollover.

part to the intended recipient's separate IRA account. This will avoid the 20 percent income tax withholding that would otherwise be required.

In a rollover, the funds are paid to the person who then remits the money to an IRA. A payment, whether or not there is a rollover, is subject to the 20 percent withholding. Only a direct transfer avoids the withholding tax.

## DEFINED-BENEFIT PLANS

A defined-benefit retirement plan promises to pay the employee a certain amount per month at retirement time. In many pensions, there are choices as to how it is to be paid out such as life, years certain, and life of employee and spouse. The value of a defined-benefit plan comes from the company's guarantee to pay based on a predetermined plan formula, not from an account balance.

For instance, the amount of monthly pension could be determined by a complex calculation that could include, in addition to the employee's final average salary, an annuity factor based on the employee's age at retirement, the employee's annual average Social Security tax base, the employee's total number of years of employment and age at retirement, the method chosen by the employee to receive payment of voluntary and required contributions, and whether a pension will be paid to a survivor upon the employee's death. As you might guess, the valuation of such a plan poses a challenge and has fostered much creativity!

Here's an example of how a defined-benefit plan works with Henry and Ginny from the previous example. Assume that based on today's earnings and his length of time with the company, Henry will receive $1,200 a month at age 65 from his pension. He is now age 56, and has to wait nine more years before he can start receiving the $1,200 per month. Because of the wait, it is called a *future benefit*. You can, though, value this future stream of income and put down a present value of what it is worth today. This present value can be used in the list of assets for purposes of dividing property.

You could, for example, divide the defined-benefit plan according to a QDRO by saying that Ginny will receive $600 when Henry retires. However, when he retires, his benefit will probably be worth more than $1,200 per month because he will have worked there longer. When Henry retires, he may get $1,800 a month, but if the QDRO states that Ginny will receive $600 per month, she won't get any more even though the value of the fund has increased.

It is important to find out whether (1) the $1,200 per month is what he will get at age 65 based on today's earnings and time with the company or (2) the $1,200 per month figure assumed is what he will get if he stays with he company until age 65 with projected earnings built in. If it is not clear on the pension statements, these questions must be asked of the plan administrator.

If the couple has less than eight years to wait until retirement, Ginny may choose to wait to get the $600 per month so she can have guaranteed income. However, if they are 9, 10, or more years away from retirement, she may wish to trade out another asset up front. This way, she'll be assured of getting some funding. The media has reported that many retirement plans have disappeared due to mismanagement of the funds or the company going out of business.

Assume that Ginny decides to wait for nine years until Henry retires to receive her benefit. They have been married for 32 years. Instead of stating in the QDRO that she will receive $600 per month, it may be more prudent to use a formula that states that she will receive a percentage (e.g., half) of the following:

$$\frac{\text{Number of years married while working}}{\text{Total number of years worked until retirement}} = \frac{32}{41}$$

If Henry's final benefit would pay him $1,800 per month

$$\frac{32}{41} \times \$1,800 \text{ divided by } 2 = \$702$$

This may be a more equitable division of the pension based on the premise that Ginny was married to Henry during the early building-up years of the plan.

It is also important to ascertain if the plan will pay Ginny at retirement time (Henry's age 65) in case Henry doesn't retire. He may decide not to retire just so Ginny can't get her portion of his retirement plan! Some companies allow the exspouse to start receiving benefits at retirement time even if the employee spouse has not retired. This depends on both the QDRO's dividing method and the plan.

## Limitations in Using a QDRO

There are too many horror stories in which a case has gone to court, everything has been settled, the QDRO has been presented to the judge, and the judge says the divorce is final. Then the QDRO is sent to the pension plan and the exspouse ends up not getting any money. Why? Because the plan doesn't have to and won't pay it.

From *Informational Guide on "QDROs" under the IBM Retirement Plan:*

> You must look at the pension documents during the divorce proceedings and before the divorce is final.

How long does it take for a plan to approve a QDRO?

The answer and our experience has been that it can take several months. This is because draft orders or orders that have been entered without our advance review often have conditions that we cannot implement or which require forms of payment which are *not allowed* under the plan. For example, we often see orders that require an immediate lump sum payment of the former spouse's total share of the benefit. Since the IBM retirement plan *does not pay* in lump sums except for accrued benefits with a present actuarial value of $3,500 or less or for PRP benefits, but pays only on a monthly basis for life, an order requiring a lump sum payment *must be rejected* and *will not be accepted* until the court has issued an order that complies with the provisions of the plan.[1] (emphasis added)

A QDRO generally may not require that the plan provide any form of benefit not otherwise provided under the plan and may not require that the plan provide increased benefits. However, within certain limits, it is

---

1. *Informational Guide on "QDROs" under the IBM Retirement Plan,* Prepared for Counsel in Domestic Relations Matters, June 1, 1991.

permissible for a QDRO to require that payments to the alternate payee begin on or after the participant's earliest retirement age, even though the participant has not retired at that time. One area of liability in drafting a QDRO for a pension plan is when the pension documents do not allow for the ex-spouse to receive benefits before the employee spouse has retired.

An expert from a pension department once said, "We will answer any question that you ask, but we will not volunteer any information." You need to ask the questions. The client doesn't really understand how to ask questions and sometimes the attorney doesn't either. You should at least call the company's pension department and ask

Do you allow a QDRO?

Will you pay it in a lump sum?

Will you separate the accounts?

Can the nonemployee spouse receive benefits before the employee spouse retires?

Pension departments won't figure the present value for you and you cannot ask specific questions about the client's account unless you have *his* or *her signature that releases such information* to you.

## Case Studies Showing Four Different Parameters of the Defined Benefit

### Case 1 (Based on Present Value as of Leaving the Company Today)

Richard will receive $2,600 per month at age 65 from his defined-benefit plan. (This is based on his years of service and earnings as of today.) He is now age 52. The life expectancy table shows that he has a life expectancy of an additional 26.9 years. So his life expectancy right now is 78.9 years. He will receive $2,600 a month times 12 (i.e., $31,200 a year). Thus,

| $31,200 | = | Payment |
| 13.9 | = | $n$ (number of years between age 65 and 78.9) |
| 5.5 | = | % interest (See the discussion below on the discount rate.) |

Now calculate PV (present value). We find that the PV is $287,758. That is the amount of money needed at age 65 to be able to pay Richard $31,200 per year for 13.9 years, which is his life expectancy after he retires.

Now calculate the present value as of today:

$287,758  =  FV (future value)
13        =  *n* (number of years until he reaches age 65)
5.5       =  % (interest rate)

We find that the present value is $148,450. That is the present value of his future stream of income. It represents the lump sum of money needed today invested at 5.5 percent to create a lump sum of money at age 65 that will pay Richard $31,200 per year for his life expectancy.

Not all states allow this method of valuation. Be sure to check your own state for guidelines and policies.

## Case 2 (Based on Present Value Assuming He Works until Age 65)

Henry and Sara have been married for 25 years. Henry has been working at his company for 20 years. He will continue to work there after they have been divorced. His defined-benefit pension plan will pay him $2,600 per month at age 65. (This is based on the assumption that he continues to work there until age 65 at his current earning level.) He is now age 52 and his life expectancy is 78.9.

The present value is exactly the same as in Case 1—$148,450. Consider that he has worked there for 20 years at this point, and he will have worked there for 33 years by the time he finishes working. The marital portion of his pension will be 20/33rds of the present value.

$$\frac{20 \times \$148,450}{32} = \$89,970$$

The present value of the marital portion of Henry's pension is $89,970.

Did you notice the differences between Case 1 and Case 2? Case 1 says that, based on today's earnings, Richard's pension is worth $2,600 per month when he retires. If he were to quit today, he would get $2,600 a month at age 65. Case 2 assumes that Henry works until age 65 to get his pension of $2,600 a month.

Again, check with your own state for acceptable methods of evaluating pensions.

## Case 3 (Based on the Same Assumptions as Case 1 and That He Works for the Company Longer than Being Married)

Larry and Sue have been married for 15 years and Larry has worked for his company for 20 years. Therefore, you know only 75 percent of that portion is marital property. Larry is now age 52 and his life expectancy is 78.9 years. Figure the present value exactly the same as before.

Now, when you look at the present value, you will take 15/20ths (i.e., 75 percent) of the present value to see what the marital portion of the pension is.

$$\frac{15}{20} \times \$148,450 = \$101,501$$

The present value of the marital portion of Larry's pension is $101,501.

Let's assume you decide to draft a QDRO for this pension so that Sue gets a portion of the monthly payment when he retires instead of looking at it as a lump-sum value. You would look at her getting 75 percent of the marital portion of the monthly payment when he retires, so you can do either a portion of the monthly payment or a portion of the present value. In this case, Sue would be getting half of 75 percent (i.e., 37 ½ percent) of $2,600.

Again, check the acceptable methods in your own state.

The calculated lump-sum value of a retirement plan depends on the assumptions you use for the data. A lot of litigation may surround this data because it can make a substantial difference in the present value. Also, your discounting assumptions can create a substantial difference. So, rather then fight about value, you just divide it "in kind." You do not care what the value is because of the percentage division. You could argue that the pension is worth $100,000 so he gets the pension and she gets the $100,000 house. Or you can just divide the pension 50/50. Again, you do not care if it is worth $150,000, $100,000 or $50,000 because you are dividing it "in kind."

## Case 4 (Based on the Pension Being Protected from Inflation)

Marvin is age 52 and plans to retire at age 65. His pension will pay him $2,600 per month based on today's earnings and years of service with the company. Marvin's pension benefit is protected from inflation and will have a cost of living adjustment each year.

To get the inflation-adjusted interest rate, we use the following formula:

$$\frac{1 + \text{Assumed discount rate}}{1 + \text{Inflation rate}} - 1 \times 100 = \text{Inflation-adjusted interest}$$

$$\frac{1 + 5.5\% - 1 \times 100}{1 + 4\%}$$

$$\frac{1.055 - 1 \times 100}{1.04}$$

$$1.014 - 1 \times 100 = 1.44$$

After Marvin starts receiving his $2,600 per month at age 65, you figure the present value using the inflation-adjusted interest rate.

| | | |
|---|---|---|
| $31,200 | = | Payment |
| 13.9 | = | Number of years between age 65 and 78.9 |
| 1.44% | = | Inflation-adjusted interest rate |
| $390,500 | = | Present value |

Between now and Marvin's retirement, we use our regular interest rate.

| | | |
|---|---|---|
| $390,500 | = | FV (future value) |
| 13 | = | Number of years until he is age 65 |
| 5.5% | = | Interest rate |
| $194,688 | = | PV |

The present value of Marvin's inflation-protected pension is $194,688.

## PUBLIC EMPLOYEES' PENSIONS

Another type of defined benefit plan is for public employees such as school teacher, principals, librarians, firemen, police, and state troopers. This type of plan typically will not allow any division by order of a QDRO in a divorce.

Each year, the employee gets a statement showing his contributions to this plan. This sum of money (plus interest) is what the employee can take if he quits or is fired. However, if the employee stays in the job for a minimum number of years (usually age 20 or 25), he or she will receive an annuity retirement payout that is a percentage of his or her final average pay. It is at retirement time that the employee sees the contribution of the company.

Janice and Frank had been married for 23 years. Frank started out as a school teacher but at the time of their divorce, he was the principal of the high school in their small city. The statement of his retirement account showed that he had paid in $82,050 and that is the number that Frank used as his value of his retirement. His attorney accepted this number.

Janice's attorney encouraged her to hire a financial expert, who determined that when Frank retires, he will get 60 percent of his final average salary, or $32,050 per year. The financial expert testified in court that the present value of the marital portion of that future stream of income is $373,060—a far cry from $82,050! The judge, after dividing all the other assets equally, declared that Frank still owed Janice $133,585, which should be paid to her via a property settlement note over 20 years at $957 per month. Frank's attorney looked more carefully at future clients' retirement plans!

## DISCOUNT RATE OF INTEREST

In figuring the present value of a future stream of income, there is a relationship between the interest rate and the present value. The higher the interest rate, the lower the present value of the pension, and vice versa.

Pension plans, when valuing their pensions, can use any rate they wish. There are many arguments.

The Pension Benefit Guaranty Corporation (PBGC), an organization in Washington, D.C., announces monthly the interest rate for figuring pension plans for the following month. This has become the reliable national standard for computing present values of pensions in divorce cases because it removes battling experts' speculation as to what interest rate to use. The PBGC's number is 202-326-4000.

The rate that many companies use for figuring the present value of a future stream of defined-benefit payments for the purpose of valuing a pension in a divorce is the lump sum rate according to the PBGC. It will be lower than the annuity rate. The lump sum rate is calculated by using average annuity prices less the commission or load. The only problem with using this lower number is that it tends to inflate the value of the pension. This creates a lot of ill will among companies who have had to pay out large sums of money at retirement to buy an annuity. They then started using the annuity rate instead of the lump sum rate.

Some states actually require the use of the lump sum rate when fig-uring the value of pensions. However, the lump sum rate tends to over-state the value of the pension of a young person, age 35 to 40.

The passage of GATT (General Agreement of Tariffs and Trade) called for the minimum interest rate being "the annual rate of interest on 30-year Treasury securities for the month before the date of distribution . . . " (Retirement Protection Act of 1994, Sec. 767(a)(2)). Companies can use the GATT rate only if their plan is amended to allow that. How-ever, GATT requires companies to amend their plans by the year 2000 to compute present values and lump-sum distributions using the GATT rate based on 30-year Treasuries. Within the coming five years, all affected plans will drop their reliance on PBGC rates and use GATT rates.

Another thing to remember is if you had valued a pension six months earlier, the interest rate might have been different.

In Colorado and many other states, the present value of a pension plan is to be figured at the earliest date of retirement that can be taken without penalty or reduction of benefit. Before this rule was established, one side's expert would say, "This is the value of his pension when he re-tires at age 65." The other side's expert would say, "But he is going to take early retirement at age 55 so this is the value of this pension in-stead." Obviously, two different values would be produced.

If a company allows retirement at the age of 60 with full bene-fits, figure the present value from that point. Make sure you verify what the law in your jurisdiction is to determine which method your state courts use.

## SURVIVOR BENEFITS

When you are dividing the defined-benefit plan, keep in mind that you must work with the plan administrator in setting up survivor benefits. You would be very unhappy if your client got 50 percent of the defined-bene-fit plan and then the employee died and the rest of the money wasn't paid out. You either need to state it simply—joint and survivor annuity—which of course will have a reduction in ultimate benefit, or you can lit-erally take your client's portion—40 percent or whatever—and have it set up in a separate account. It will all be calculated and annualized at the time of payment. That way, your client gets it whether or not the em-ployee dies, and you are not choosing a joint and survivor annuity. This is only true after the alternate payee starts receiving his or her share. Make sure that (1) you understand the plan, (2) there are options available in the event of the employee's death, and (3) you have included them in your planning.

For example, an ex-wife can preserve her right to receive survivor's benefits if her husband should die before retirement. This means that, before he can waive such coverage, an ex-husband must obtain his ex-wife's written consent and have it notarized, *even if he has remarried and wants his new spouse to receive the benefits instead.* A divorce decree that earmarks the money for a former spouse can override the rights of a subsequent spouse.

## VESTING

Vesting refers to the employee's entitlement to retirement benefits. A participant is vested when he or she has an immediate, fixed right to present or future enjoyment of the accrued benefit. The percentage of vesting means the percentage of what the employee is entitled to from the retirement plan when he or she retires, quits, or is fired.

When *fully vested,* an employee is entitled to all the benefits that the employer has contributed. Being *partially vested* means that if the employee quit the job, he or she would be able to take that percentage of the employer's contributions. For example, if the employee was 30 percent vested and the employer's contributions were $1,500, the employee could take $450.

Any contributions made by the employee to the plan are immediately 100 percent vested. The employee is always entitled to take all of his contributions plus the earnings on those contributions.

An employee must be given nonforfeitable rights to his accrued benefits derived from employer contributions in accordance with *one* of the following two vesting schedules:

**1.** *Five-year cliff vesting.* An employee who has at least five years of service must have a nonforfeitable right to 100 percent of his accrued benefit. (See IRC Sec. 411(a)(2)(A).)

**2.** *3/7 vesting.* An employee who has completed at least three years of service must have a nonforfeitable right to at least the following percentages of his accrued benefit: 20 percent after 3 years of service, 40 percent after 4 years of service, 60 percent after 5 years of service, 80 percent after 6 years of service, and 100 percent after 7 years of service. (See IRC Sec. 411(a)(2)(B).)

It is important at divorce to find out whether the state considers nonvested retirement benefits to be marital property. If so, a defined contribution plan's total value could be divided, and the employee could leave his job and never receive the nonvested amounts.

For example, Marvin worked for ABC, Inc. His 401(k) was worth $58,000, which was made up of $12,300 from his contributions and $45,700 from his employer's contributions. Marvin is 40 percent vested. If he quit his job today, he could take his own $12,300 and $18,280 of his employer's contributions for a total of $30,580. He and his exwife Susie agreed to value his 401(k) at the full $58,000 for purposes of dividing property. Marvin kept his 401(k) and paid Susie $29,000 for her half out of the savings account money. Six months after the divorce was final, ABC, Inc., laid off half its workforce including Marvin. He left the company with $30,580 from his retirement account. The net result was that he ended up $13,710 short in the division of marital property.

## MATURE PLANS

An employee may be fully vested but may still have to wait until he or she reaches a certain age before being able to receive any benefits. For instance, some companies do not pay out benefits until the employee has reached age 60 or age 65. And in some cases, if the employee is not vested in the plan and dies before retirement age, the benefits are lost. Nobody gets them.

> You can divide the plan or divide the stream of income, but do not divide both.

## DOUBLE DIPPING

Sometimes a retirement plan is divided at divorce as part of the property division. Then, when the employee retires, his income from his portion of the retirement plan is considered when calculating alimony and/or child support. The end result is that the nonemployee spouse is getting paid twice from the same asset. What is used as income in determining alimony depends on state law.

## THE CARROT STORY

Understanding how defined-benefit pensions really work is often confusing to even the most knowledgeable financial experts. The following excerpt from *Assigning Retirement Benefits in Divorce* by Gale S. Finley is a delightful way to learn the ins and outs of defined-benefit plans.

\*       \*       \*       \*

Imagine a farm in central Kentucky that raises race horses. The owner of the farm takes his racing very seriously and comes up with a way to reward his horses for winning races for him. He calls it the "Carrot Retirement Plan." He decides that after each horse retires from racing, it will be provided an allocation of carrots each week as a supplement to its regular diet. The number of carrots a horse receives each week depends upon the number of races it wins during its racing career. Each horse will receive its weekly allotment of carrots until it goes to that big pasture in the sky.

In order to ensure an adequate supply of carrots for his retiring horses, the owner decides to plan ahead and start growing and freezing carrots. He sits down with the veterinarian and the two of them decide how many carrots he will have to grow and store each week. They look at how many horses he has, how many races each has won, when each is expected to retire, and how long each is expected to live after retirement. Based upon those initial projections, the owner comes up with a quantity of carrots that will be needed to be planted that first year. He hires an expert in carrot growing—the Keeper of the Carrots—to maintain a carrot crop that will continue to produce an adequate supply to meet future carrot obligations.

The next year the owner again sits down with his veterinarian and the Keeper of the Carrots. The owner and the veterinarian discuss factors bearing on the number of carrots that will be needed for all the retiring horses down the road, such as any new horses acquired during the year, any that have died during the year, how many races each has won, and how many will be retiring. Also, they reevaluate their projections from the previous year concerning all those same factors based upon what actually occurred during the year. The Keeper of the Carrots then reports on how well the carrot crop came in during the year and whether it will be adequate given the number of carrots the owner has projected under the Carrot Retirement Plan. They also discuss the number of carrots that will have to be planted during the next year.

Each year these three people sit down and look at the events that have occurred during the year and how those events affect future carrot obligations. The goal is always for the three of them to work together to ensure that, at retirement, each horse is given its proper weekly allotment of carrots for as long as it lives. If during a given year fewer horses than were projected are retiring, more retiring horses died than were expected to, some horses died while still active, and/or the Keeper of the Carrots brought in a bumper crop, fewer, if any, new carrots have to be planted. On the other hand, negative results as compared to the projections mean more carrots than expected must be planted.

Let's look at one of the horses covered under the Carrot Retirement Plan (the "Participant Horse"). This Participant Horse is still actively racing and occasionally winning. In addition, he has won enough races through today's date to be entitled to receive 10 carrots each week of his life beginning on the date he is permanently turned out to pasture (its "Accrued Carrot Benefit"). What can we say about this horse's rights under the Carrot Retirement Plan as of today's date? What the Participant Horse has today is a right to receive 10 carrots each week for life beginning at some future date. If he wins more races in the future, the weekly number of carrots to which he is entitled will increase. But as of today, 10 per week is the number. Remember though, it is a current right to receive carrots in the future if the Participant Horse lives long enough to receive them. The Participant Horse does not "own" any carrots. Because he is still racing, he is not currently entitled to any carrots. In fact, because he may die before he retires, he may never be entitled to receive any carrots. The owner of the horse farm owns thousands of carrots that are being stored to someday give the Participant Horse and all his co-retirees a certain number of carrots each week for their respective lives. But the Participant Horse does not own any carrots until he actually receives his first weekly allotment.

Assuming another horse—the "A-P Horse"—wants to lay claim to 50 percent of the Participant Horse's Accrued Carrot Benefit, what do we have to divide? We have the Participant Horse's right to receive 10 carrots per week for his life beginning when he retires. We can split that down the middle so that the A-P Horse will get five carrots from each 10-carrot allotment as it is distributed to the Participant Horse during his lifetime. That is the easiest way to make the division because the number of carrots to be given, the beginning date, and the ending date are already determined. No muss and no fuss.

As simple as that method may be, however, it means that the A-P Horse has absolutely no control over any aspect of the carrot distribution process. The A-P Horse may want to start receiving her carrots sooner or later than the Participant Horse's retirement date. The A-P Horse may want the security of knowing the carrots will keep coming during *her* lifetime rather than the lifetime of the Participant Horse (rumor has it the Participant Horse's health is deteriorating). Can we simply provide that the A-P Horse will receive five carrots each week during her life, beginning when she chooses? We can't if our goal is to give the A-P Horse a right to only 50 percent of the Participant Horse's Accrued Carrot Benefit as of today's date.

To understand that, let's look at what the Participant Horse's Accrued Carrot Benefit roughly translates to. We will assume that the Participant Horse will be retired in two years and will start receiving 10 carrots each week beginning November 1 of that year. At that time the Participant Horse will have a life expectancy of 20 years. If these assumptions hold true, the owner will need to be prepared to provide 10,400 carrots (10 carrots × 52 weeks × 20 years) to the Participant Horse over his lifetime. If we assume a 50/50 split of the amount so that the Participant Horse receives only five carrots per week, the lifetime total becomes 5,200 carrots.

Now let's assume the A-P Horse, because of an age difference, has a current life expectancy of 24 years. If the A-P Horse starts to receive five carrots per week (based upon the 50 percent assignment) starting now (assuming this is the "earliest retirement age") and continuing for the assumed 24 years, she will receive an aggregate of 6,240 carrots over her lifetime. This is substantially more than the 5,200 that represent 50 percent of the Accrued Carrot Benefit. Moreover, when added to the 5,200 the owner expects to give to the Participant Horse, the total (11,440) is significantly higher than the 10,400 that would be given (if all assumptions are accurate) to the Participant Horse if no assignment is made. Since a predicted 10,400 is all the owner is obligated for under the Carrot Retirement Plan, something has to give.

If, in fact, the intent of the parties is to give the A-P Horse during her lifetime the *equivalent* of 5,200 carrots over the lifetime of the Participant Horse, a couple of options exist. As we mentioned earlier, the A-P

Horse can receive half of the Participant Horse's weekly allotment of carrots while the Participant Horse is alive. But to keep carrots coming to the A-P Horse after the Participant Horse dies, she can also require the Carrot Retirement Plan to continue to deliver to her the same weekly allotment. Of course, in order to "fund" her continuing carrot supply after the death of the Participant Horse, the Carrot Retirement Plan will need to reduce the number of weekly carrots that are given out while the Participant Horse is alive. For example, it would be incorrect to give out 10 carrots per week (five to the Participant Horse and five to the A-P Horse, who is expected to live longer than the Participant Horse), upon the death of the Participant Horse (assuming she fulfills her life expectancy). Another option is for the A-P Horse to be treated as though she has her own Accrued Carrot Benefit and to receive some smaller number per week beginning when she chooses and continuing for as long as *she* lives. In our example, the latter option would result in the A-P Horse immediately beginning to receive 4,167 (5,200 divided by 24 years divided by 52 weeks) per week for her lifetime.

Either of these two options provides the A-P Horse the equivalent of 50 percent of the Participant Horse's Accrued Carrot Benefit because it ends up, if all life expectancy assumptions for the Participant Horse and the A-P Horse hold true, to be the same aggregate number of carrots the Participant Horse will receive during his life.[2]

## PITFALLS IN DIVIDING PENSIONS IN DIVORCE

Edwin C. Schilling III, J.D., is in private practice in Denver, Colorado. He is among the nation's most knowledgeable divorce attorneys on the financial and legal aspects of divorce involving military retired pay and federal civil service pensions. Mr. Schilling co-authored the Air Force position paper on proposed legislation to divide military retired pay incident to divorce. He has testified before Congress concerning national divorce legislation and is a frequent nationwide speaker on the more complex issues of divorce law. He shares some of his expertise in this area.

*       *       *       *

---

2. Gale S. Finley, *Assigning Retirement Benefits in Divorce: A Practical Guide to Negotiating and Drafting QDROs,* American Bar Association, 1995), pp. 17–21.

Many mistakes are being made when Qualified Domestic Relations Orders (QDROs) are drafted to divide pensions. These mistakes could result in a nonemployee spouse not getting the benefits that were anticipated.

In lawyer's filing cabinets around the country, there are thousands of ticking time bombs waiting to go off. Many errors won't be discovered for years to come—when the employee retires or dies. Errors are not limited to an incorrect division of the pension; they also include the survivor benefits.

In addition, technical errors are often made that result in a pension plan rejecting the QDRO and requiring that it be resubmitted. These errors can occur on both defined-benefit and defined-contribution plans. However, the most common mistakes are with defined-benefit plans because they are more complex.

Here are the biggest mistakes to be aware of.

## Failing to Anticipate Death

The single biggest mistake is failing to address what will happen if either party dies *before* the nonemployee gets the whole share of the pension. A QDRO can either miss this issue completely or get it wrong.

***What If the Employee Dies?***   Almost all pension plans provide for death benefits in case an employee dies *before* retirement. However, a nonemployee former spouse can't share in these benefits unless the QDRO specifically provides for this. A court order must award either a dollar amount or a percentage of the death benefits, or the former spouse won't get anything when the employee dies. Frequently overlooked is the possibility that the QDRO could order the plan to treat the former spouse as a surviving spouse for the purposes of this protection.

There is a similar problem if the employee dies *after* retirement. ERISA says that a spouse is always entitled to a survivor annuity unless it is waived. But this isn't true for an *ex*-spouse. The only way to provide an exspouse with a survivor annuity is to spell it out specifically in the QDRO.

Another alternative to naming the ex-spouse as the recipient of the survivor annuity is to have the plan divide the account when the employee retires, and use a portion of this account to fund a lifetime annuity for the nonemployee. This can be a good idea if the employee plans to remarry, since the employee will still have the option of providing a new spouse with a survivor annuity.

**What If the Nonemployee Dies?**   If the nonemployee dies before the receipt of the pension benefits, it is often assumed that the funds will pass to the nonemployee's estate. This is not necessarily true. With some plans, it is not possible; with other plans, it has to be specifically provided for. If the QDRO has no language about what happens if the nonemployee should die, the plan would probably take the position that it doesn't know whom to pay, and the plan would absorb the account.

## Not Understanding Plan Provisions and Features

A big problem is drafting a QDRO without knowing what the plan provides. It's hard to negotiate what is best for your client if you don't know what is available. It is important to always obtain at least a copy of the summary plan description.

Normally, a nonemployee won't start receiving benefits until the employee does, but many pension plans permit a nonemployee to start receiving payments as of the employee's earliest possible retirement date. Also, many 401(k) plans permit an immediate distribution or transfer into another qualified plan or IRA at the time of divorce.

In addition, many lawyers don't understand that QDROs only apply to qualified plans under ERISA. They try to prepare a QDRO for a government plan that has its own set of rules.

Two other common errors result from a failure to understand the plan:

- Lawyers request a lump sum when it is not provided for in the plan.
- When dealing with a defined-benefit plan, many QDROs ask for a division of the account balance as of the date of the divorce decree. But most plans still don't value their accounts on a daily basis. If the plan only values its accounts on a quarterly basis, then the pension plan cannot administer the order and it will be rejected.

## Finalizing the Divorce before the QDRO Is Approved

The QDRO should be approved by the pension plan *before* the divorce is final. This is because the nonemployee is unprotected during the period between the divorce and QDRO approval. If the employee retires, dies, or remarries in the interim, the nonemployee may well end up with nothing.

These scenarios should be considered:

- *If the employee retires,* a single-life annuity could be chosen and the nonemployee exspouse's right to a survivor annuity would be lost.

- *If the employee dies,* the nonemployee exspouse won't get any death benefits because the nonemployee is no longer a "spouse," and there is not yet a QDRO requiring the plan to make payments. As long as they are married, if the employee dies, the spouse is automatically the beneficiary under ERISA unless the option was waived.

- *If the employee remarries,* the nonemployee ex-spouse may have trouble obtaining a death benefit or a survivor annuity in the QDRO. This is because it may be unclear whether rights of the nonemployee's former spouse supersede those of the new spouse. Once the marriage is terminated and there is a new spouse, it may be very difficult to get a fair order.

## Relying Only on Forms Provided by the Plan

It can be a big mistake to simply rely on a sample QDRO form provided by the plan administrator as it will often favor the plan or employee. For example, the form might state that the nonemployee can't share in any retirement bonus the employee gets, or might simply not raise the bonus issue at all.

Drafters need to consider whether the language in the sample order is better for their client or better for the other party. If they don't consider this, they may not be getting the client all he or she is entitled to. It's worthwhile to obtain a model order that would be acceptable, but don't treat that as the only possibility.

## Failing to Divide an Early Retirement Bonus

Some retirement plans offer a substantial bonus to employees who retire early. Consideration should be given to negotiating for a portion of it, or not dividing it in exchange for some concession or property.

## Not Having the QDRO Pre-Approved by the Plan Administrator

Whenever possible, one should obtain a pre-approval of a QDRO to avoid embarrassing mistakes. Most plan administrators gladly help at this stage because it avoids problems later. Getting a QDRO pre-approved saves the embarrassment of having the order rejected and having to go back to the judge for a revision.

## RAMIFICATIONS OF DIVIDING A 401(k) PLAN

Ron and Nancy have been married 20 years and have two sons, ages 8 and 5. Ron is 43 years old. He has take-home pay of $51,098 per year and expenses of $25,980 per year. He will retire at age 65.

Nancy is also 43 years old and works at the town library. She brings home $13,500 per year and has expenses of $35,676 per year with the two boys. Nancy wants custody of their sons.

Table 6–1 shows the proposed settlement. We'll call this scenario 1.

- Nancy will keep her car and some of the furniture. She will receive custody of the sons and will get child support of $967 per month ($11,600 per year) until their oldest son is 19 years old. At this point, child support will decrease to $7,500 per year until the youngest son reaches 19 years of age. This is in accordance with the child support guidelines in their state. Nancy will receive $172,975 in retirement benefits (401(k) and IRA funds) and $30,000 from a certificate of deposit.

- Ron feels that since Nancy is getting $172,975 in retirement benefits, she does not need alimony.

- Ron will keep their house and Nancy will buy a new house with her part of the CD.

- Ron will also keep his car and some furniture. He will take his pension, part of the certificate of deposit, and $123,525 in retirement benefits.

This settlement represents a 50/50 split of the marital assets as shown in Table 6–1. Look at the table. The net equity in the home, $27,700, is in Ron's column. The household goods were split according to what each of them wanted for their homes. They each took their own car. Notice that the remainder of their assets except for the CD are in retirement plans such as the 401(k), IRAs, and the pension. While each party is getting 50 percent of the assets, is it really an equitable settlement?

Even though they have split their assets 50/50, the majority of their assets are in retirement accounts. Let's look at the final result.

**TABLE 6 - 1**

Ron and Nancy Asset Table 1 (50/50)

| Item | Value | Nancy | Ron |
|------|-------|-------|-----|
| Home (net) | $ 27,700 | | $ 27,700 |
| Household goods | 8,500 | $ 2,500 | 6,000 |
| Automobiles | 7,000 | 1,500 | 5,500 |
| 401(k) | 252,700 | 154,475 | 98,225 |
| Ron's IRA | 25,300 | | 25,300 |
| Nancy's IRA | 18,500 | 18,500 | |
| Pension | 32,500 | | 32,500 |
| Certificate of deposit | 41,750 | 30,000 | 11,750 |
| Total | $413,950 | $206,975 | $206,975 |
| Down payment on house | | (25,000) | |
| Working capital column | | 5,000 | 11,750 |
| Retirement asset column | | 172,975 | 123,525 |

Table 6–2 is Nancy's spreadsheet for scenario 1. The first column shows the year—it starts with 1996. The second column shows Nancy's age, 43. The next three columns are income columns as indicated by the bracket above them labeled "Income." The "Take-Home Pay" column shows her *after-tax* take-home pay. The 4 percent indicates that it is increasing at 4 percent per year. A 4 percent increase is factored in for inflation in this case study. Nancy's income just keeps up with inflation. If inflation were estimated at 5 percent, her income increase should be illustrated at 5 percent.

The next column is labeled "Child Support." Nancy will receive $11,600 per year in child support for 11 years until their 8-year-old son turns age 19. At that time child support will decrease to $7,500 per year until the 5-year-old is 19.

The next column, "Maintenance Support," has no dollar amounts in it. Ron does not want to pay any maintenance. Therefore, this scenario's financial result will be for both of them if no maintenance is paid.

The next four columns are under the bracket labeled "Expenses." The first two columns ("Living Expenses" and "Real Estate Payments") together equal her living expenses. They are separated into two columns

## TABLE 6 - 2

## Nancy's Spreadsheet (Scenario 1)

| Year | Age | Income: Take-Home Pay 4.0% $13,500 | Income: Child Support 11 $11,600 | Income: Maint. Support 8 | Expenses: Living Expenses 4.0% $35,676 | Expenses: Real Estate Payments 30 $555 | Expenses: Other Expenses | Expenses: Taxes on Maint. | Annual Net Cash Flow | Working Capital 5.0% $5,000 | Retirement Accounts 8.0% $172,975 | Fair Market Value Real Estate 4.0% $100,000 | Real Estate Mortgage 30 8.0% $75,000 | Net Worth |
|---|---|---|---|---|---|---|---|---|---|---|---|---|---|---|
| 1996 | 43 | $13,500 | $11,600 | | $29,014 | $6,662 | | | ($10,576) | | $177,980 | $104,000 | $74,338 | $207,642 |
| 1997 | 44 | 14,040 | 11,600 | | 30,175 | 6,662 | | | (11,197) | | 173,651 | 108,160 | 73,623 | 208,188 |
| 1988 | 45 | 14,602 | 11,600 | | 31,382 | 6,662 | | | (11,842) | | 167,904 | 112,486 | 72,851 | 207,540 |
| 1999 | 46 | 15,186 | 11,600 | | 32,637 | 6,662 | | | (12,513) | | 160,585 | 116,986 | 72,017 | 205,554 |
| 2000 | 47 | 15,793 | 11,600 | | 33,942 | 6,662 | | | (13,211) | | 151,523 | 121,665 | 71,116 | 202,072 |
| 2001 | 48 | 16,425 | 11,600 | | 35,300 | 6,662 | | | (13,937) | | 140,531 | 126,532 | 70,143 | 196,920 |
| 2002 | 49 | 17,082 | 11,600 | | 36,712 | 6,662 | | | (14,692) | | 127,409 | 131,593 | 69,093 | 189,909 |
| 2003 | 50 | 17,765 | 11,600 | | 38,180 | 6,662 | | | (15,477) | | 111,934 | 136,857 | 67,958 | 180,833 |
| 2004 | 51 | 18,476 | 11,600 | | 39,708 | 6,662 | | | (16,294) | | 93,867 | 142,331 | 66,733 | 169,466 |
| 2005 | 52 | 19,215 | 11,600 | | 41,296 | 6,662 | | | (17,143) | | 72,946 | 148,024 | 65,409 | 155,562 |
| 2006 | 53 | 19,983 | 11,600 | | 42,948 | 6,662 | ($4,100) | | (18,027) | | 48,887 | 153,945 | 63,980 | 138,853 |
| 2007 | 54 | 20,783 | 7,500 | | 40,566 | 6,662 | | | (18,945) | | 21,380 | 160,103 | 62,436 | 119,047 |
| 2008 | 55 | 21,614 | 7,500 | | 42,188 | 6,662 | | | (19,736) | ($5,813) | | 166,507 | 60,769 | 99,926 |
| 2009 | 56 | 22,478 | 7,500 | | 43,876 | 6,662 | (7,500) | | (20,599) | (26,372) | | 173,168 | 58,968 | 87,827 |
| 2010 | 57 | 23,378 | | | 38,131 | 6,662 | | | (21,415) | (47,788) | | 180,094 | 57,024 | 75,283 |
| 2011 | 58 | 24,313 | | | 39,656 | 6,662 | | | (22,005) | (69,793) | | 187,298 | 54,924 | 62,581 |
| 2012 | 59 | 25,285 | | | 41,242 | 6,662 | | | (22,619) | (92,412) | | 194,790 | 52,655 | 49,722 |
| 2013 | 60 | 26,297 | | | 42,892 | 6,662 | | | (23,257) | (115,670) | | 202,582 | 50,206 | 36,706 |
| 2014 | 61 | 27,349 | | | 44,608 | 6,662 | | | (23,921) | (139,591) | | 210,685 | 47,560 | 23,533 |
| 2015 | 62 | 28,442 | | | 46,392 | 6,662 | | | (24,612) | (164,203) | | 219,112 | 44,703 | 10,206 |
| 2016 | 63 | 29,580 | | | 48,248 | 6,662 | | | (25,330) | (189,533) | | 227,877 | 41,617 | (3,273) |

because the "Real Estate Payments" column represents the principal and interest (P&I) payment only. It is not affected by inflation. Taxes and insurance (T&I) are reflected in the "Living Expenses" column. If the P&I were included in the living expenses column, that number, affected by inflation, would eventually become skewed. Therefore, the $35,676 above the line is her total yearly living expense, which is a combination of the two numbers below the line: $29,014 plus $6,662 for 1996.

The "Other Expenses" column reflects any changes in Nancy's living expenses. It can be used to illustrate any expenses increasing or added (such as going back to school) and then decreasing (as when she finishes school). It can be used to show debt being paid off, which will lower her living expenses. Nancy's scenario shows a negative $4,100 in the year 2007 and a negative $7,500 in the year 2010. These numbers represent the years after both sons turn age 19 and leave home. At that time, child support stops. The assumption is that Nancy no longer has the expenses associated with that child so corresponding living expenses will be reduced by that amount.

The column labeled "Taxes on Maintenance" has no dollar amounts in it. This scenario does not allow for maintenance. The next column, "Annual Net Cash Flow," shows whether there is positive or negative cash flow after netting the income columns with the expense columns. Nancy has a negative $10,576 in the first year, meaning her expenses exceed her income by $10,576.

The number from the "Annual Net Cash Flow" column is automatically subtracted from (or added to if it is a positive number) the next column, "Working Capital." Notice that Nancy's "Working Capital" column started out with $5,000, which was in Table 6–1's asset table. This is what remained from her CD after the down payment made on her house. This asset was depleted in the first year to help cover her negative cash flow.

The next column shows her retirement accounts earning an average of 8 percent before tax. When the "Working Capital" column is exhausted, the "Retirement Accounts" column will automatically cover the negative cash flow *less taxes and penalties* if she is under the age of 60. After age 60, taxes are deducted. Notice that this depletes her "Retirement Accounts" column rather quickly.

Because she pays 28 percent federal tax, 5 percent state tax, and 10 percent penalty for early withdrawal, Nancy has to take out *43 percent more than she needs* to cover her negative cash flow. Judges and attorneys know this rule but they don't understand the real impact it has on the bottom line.

At age 54, Nancy's spendable assets have been depleted. She still owns the house, but she can't use the house to buy groceries.

The next column, "Fair Market Value Real Estate," shows the value of the $100,000 home that Nancy just bought. The 4 percent represents the average increase in real estate in her part of her city over the past 10 years. The "Real Estate Mortgage" column carries the $75,000 mortgage on Nancy's home which she took out for 30 years at 8 percent interest.

The final column, "Net Worth," is a combination of "Working Capital" plus "Retirement Accounts" plus "Fair Market Value Real Estate" minus "Real Estate Mortgage." Figure 6–1 graphs net worth. But before discussing it, let's look at Ron's spreadsheet to see how this scenario 1 affects him financially.

As Table 6–3 shows, Ron's take-home pay is $51,098 and is increasing at 4 percent per year, the same as Nancy's. The "Retire" column (an income column) includes any monies he receives from his pension after he retires. Ron will start receiving $39,924 per year after retirement at age 65.

The next two columns, "Living Expenses" and "Real Estate Payments," include his total living expenses: $17,343 plus $8,637 equal $25,980. The "Child Support" column is the amount that he pays. The "Annual Net Cash Flow" column has a positive $13,518 in the first year. This is added to the "Working Capital" column which is shown earning an average of 5 percent per year after taxes.

The "Retirement Accounts" column shows $123,525 that he received (as shown in Table 6–1), earning an average of 8 percent per year before tax. The "Fair Market Value Real Estate" reflects the value of his $105,000 home increasing at 4 percent per year. The "Real Estate Mortgage" column shows that he has 26 years left to pay on his $77,300 mortgage at 10.3 percent interest. Ron's "Net Worth" column is a combination of "Working Capital" plus "Retirement Accounts" plus "Fair Market Value Real Estate" minus "Real Estate Mortgage."

Figure 6–1 graphs Ron and Nancy's net worth based on the previous assumptions. Why is the result of this divorce settlement so uneven when we divided the assets equally? The answer, again, comes down to the disparity in earning potential. In the early years of their marriage,

Ron and Nancy's Scenario 1 Graph

**Net Worth**

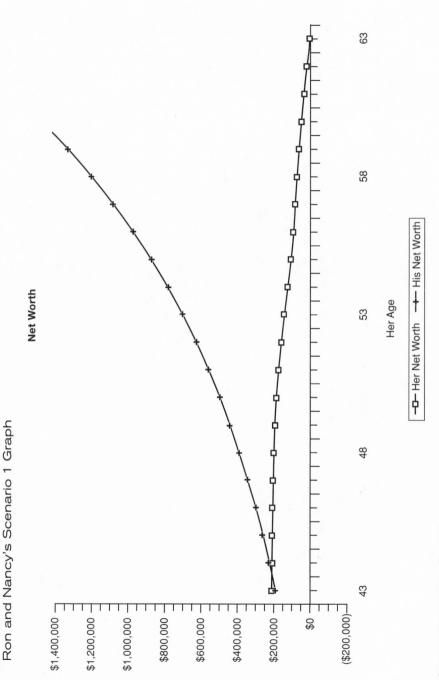

# TABLE 6-3

## Ron's Spreadsheet (Scenario 1)

| | | Income | | Expenses | | | | | Annual | Working | Retirement | Fair Market Value | Real Estate | Net |
| | | Take-Home Pay | Retire at 65 | Living Expenses | Real Estate Payments | Other Expenses | Child Support | Maint. Support | Net Cash Flow | Capital | Accounts | Real Estate | Mortgage | Worth |
| Year | Age | 4.0% | | 4.0% | 26 | 26 | | | | 5.0% | 8.0% | 4.0% | 26 10.3% | |
| 1996 | 43 | $51,098 | $39,924 | $25,980 | $720 | $720 | | | $13,518 | $11,750 | $123,525 | $105,000 | $77,300 | $191,838 |
|---|---|---|---|---|---|---|---|---|---|---|---|---|---|---|
| 1996 | 43 | $ 51,098 | | $17,343 | $8,637 | | $11,600 | | $13,518 | $ 25,855 | $133,407 | $109,200 | $76,625 | $ 191,838 |
| 1997 | 44 | 53,142 | | 18,037 | 8,637 | | 11,600 | | 14,868 | 42,016 | 144,080 | 113,568 | 75,880 | 223,784 |
| 1998 | 45 | 55,268 | | 18,758 | 8,637 | | 11,600 | | 16,272 | 60,390 | 155,606 | 118,111 | 75,059 | 259,047 |
| 1999 | 46 | 57,478 | | 19,509 | 8,637 | | 11,600 | | 17,733 | 81,142 | 168,054 | 122,835 | 74,153 | 297,879 |
| 2000 | 47 | 59,777 | | 20,289 | 8,637 | | 11,600 | | 19,252 | 104,450 | 181,499 | 127,749 | 73,153 | 340,544 |
| 2001 | 48 | 62,169 | | 21,100 | 8,637 | | 11,600 | | 20,831 | 130,504 | 196,019 | 132,858 | 72,051 | 387,330 |
| 2002 | 49 | 64,655 | | 21,944 | 8,637 | | 11,600 | | 22,474 | 159,503 | 211,700 | 138,173 | 70,835 | 438,541 |
| 2003 | 50 | 67,241 | | 22,822 | 8,637 | | 11,600 | | 24,182 | 191,660 | 228,636 | 143,700 | 69,494 | 494,502 |
| 2004 | 51 | 69,931 | | 23,735 | 8,637 | | 11,600 | | 25,959 | 227,202 | 246,927 | 149,448 | 68,015 | 555,562 |
| 2005 | 52 | 72,728 | | 24,684 | 8,637 | | 11,600 | | 27,807 | 266,369 | 266,681 | 155,426 | 66,384 | 622,092 |
| 2006 | 53 | 75,638 | | 25,672 | 8,637 | | 11,600 | | 29,729 | 309,416 | 288,016 | 161,643 | 64,584 | 694,490 |
| 2007 | 54 | 78,663 | | 26,699 | 8,637 | | 7,500 | | 35,827 | 360,714 | 311,057 | 168,108 | 62,599 | 777,280 |
| 2008 | 55 | 81,810 | | 27,767 | 8,367 | | 7,500 | | 37,906 | 416,656 | 335,942 | 174,833 | 60,410 | 867,020 |
| 2009 | 56 | 85,082 | | 28,877 | 8,637 | | 7,500 | | 40,068 | 477,556 | 362,817 | 181,826 | 57,995 | 964,204 |
| 2010 | 57 | 88,485 | | 30,032 | 8,637 | | | | 49,816 | 551,250 | 391,842 | 189,099 | 55,332 | 1,076,859 |
| 2011 | 58 | 92,025 | | 31,234 | 8,637 | | | | 52,154 | 630,966 | 423,190 | 196,663 | 52,394 | 1,198,425 |
| 2012 | 59 | 95,706 | | 32,483 | 8,637 | | | | 54,585 | 717,100 | 457,045 | 204,530 | 49,153 | 1,329,521 |
| 2013 | 60 | 99,534 | | 33,782 | 8,637 | | | | 57,114 | 810,069 | 493,608 | 212,711 | 45,579 | 1,470,809 |
| 2014 | 61 | 103,515 | | 35,134 | 8,637 | | | | 59,744 | 910,317 | 533,097 | 221,219 | 41,637 | 1,622,996 |
| 2015 | 62 | 107,656 | | 36,539 | 8,637 | | | | 62,480 | 1,018,312 | 575,745 | 230,068 | 37,288 | 1,786,837 |
| 2016 | 63 | 111,962 | | 38,001 | 8,637 | | | | 65,324 | 1,134,552 | 621,804 | 239,271 | 32,492 | 1,963,135 |

they decided that Nancy would raise the children and not go back to work until the children were in school. Because of this, Nancy was out of the work force for several years. Her career didn't develop as Ron's did.

Let's go on to Scenario 1–A in Table 6–4. It shows what many judges and attorneys think will happen. Again, they are aware of the rule about paying taxes and penalties when withdrawing retirement money before the age of 59 ½, but they don't understand the full impact. They think that it will look like the chart represented in Figure 6–2.

Notice that the "Retirement Accounts" column earns at the rate of 8 percent and covers the negative cash flow. It is not reduced for taxes and penalties. The amount of money reflected in the retirement account lasts until she is about 65 years of age instead of being depleted at age 54. But this scenario is not accurate! The taxes and penalties must be taken into account.

What change can be made in scenario 1 to make this a more equitable settlement? Look at the spreadsheet for scenario 2 shown in Table 6–5. It shows the result of Nancy receiving maintenance. In the "Maintenance Support" column, $1,250 per month ($15,000 per year) is included for five years. It is then reduced to $1,000 per month ($12,000 per year) for the next five years. The "Taxes on Maintenance" column reflects the taxes that she pays on this additional income. With the adjustment in maintenance payments, she has positive cash flow for five years, which enables her working capital to grow slightly before she exhausts it at age 51. At that time, she can withdraw money from her "Retirement Accounts" column, but it has a higher value than before and can support her for a much longer time.

How does paying this maintenance affect Ron? Turn to Table 6–6, which is Ron's spreadsheet. Look at his "Maintenance Support" column. Since maintenance is deductible from Ron's taxable income, the numbers in this column reflect the *after-tax* cost to him of paying Nancy maintenance. Figure 6–3 graphs scenario 2.

Paying maintenance to Nancy enables her to conserve retirement assets until she is nearly 70 years of age instead of depleting them by age 54. Ron's annual net cash flow isn't quite as large as when he paid no maintenance, but he can still increase his net worth at a healthy rate. The result shown in scenario 2 is much more equitable than that shown in scenario 1.

# TABLE 6-4

## Nancy's Spreadsheet (Scenario 1-A)

| | | Income | | | Expenses | | | | Annual | Working | Retirement | Fair Market Value | Real Estate | Net |
| | | Take-Home Pay | Child Support | Maint. Support | Living Expenses | Real Estate Payments | Other Expenses | Taxes on Maint. | Net Cash Flow | Capital | Accounts | Real Estate | Mortgage 30 | Worth |
| Year 1996 | Age 43 | 4.0% $13,500 | 11 $11,600 | 8 | 4.0% $35,676 | 30 $555 | | | | 5.0% $5,000 | 8.0% $172,975 | 4.0% $100,000 | 8.0% $75,000 | |
|---|---|---|---|---|---|---|---|---|---|---|---|---|---|---|
| 1996 | 43 | $13,500 | $11,600 | | $29,014 | $6,662 | | | ($10,576) | | $181,237 | $104,000 | $74,338 | $210,899 |
| 1997 | 44 | 14,040 | 11,600 | | 30,175 | 6,662 | | | (11,197) | | 184,539 | 108,160 | 73,623 | 219,076 |
| 1988 | 45 | 14,602 | 11,600 | | 31,382 | 6,662 | | | (11,842) | | 187,460 | 112,486 | 72,851 | 227,096 |
| 1999 | 46 | 15,186 | 11,600 | | 32,637 | 6,662 | | | (12,513) | | 189,944 | 116,986 | 72,017 | 234,913 |
| 2000 | 47 | 15,793 | 11,600 | | 33,942 | 6,662 | | | (13,211) | | 191,929 | 121,665 | 71,116 | 242,478 |
| 2001 | 48 | 16,425 | 11,600 | | 35,300 | 6,662 | | | (13,937) | | 193,346 | 126,532 | 70,143 | 249,735 |
| 2002 | 49 | 17,082 | 11,600 | | 36,712 | 6,662 | | | (14,692) | | 194,122 | 131,593 | 69,093 | 256,623 |
| 2003 | 50 | 17,765 | 11,600 | | 38,180 | 6,662 | | | (15,477) | | 194,175 | 136,857 | 67,958 | 263,074 |
| 2004 | 51 | 18,476 | 11,600 | | 39,708 | 6,662 | | | (16,294) | | 193,415 | 142,331 | 66,733 | 269,014 |
| 2005 | 52 | 19,215 | 11,600 | | 41,296 | 6,662 | | | (17,143) | | 191,745 | 148,024 | 65,409 | 274,360 |
| 2006 | 53 | 19,983 | 11,600 | | 42,948 | 6,662 | | | (18,027) | | 189,058 | 153,945 | 63,980 | 279,024 |
| 2007 | 54 | 20,783 | 7,500 | | 40,566 | 6,662 | ($4,100) | | (18,945) | | 185,238 | 160,103 | 62,436 | 282,905 |
| 2008 | 55 | 21,614 | 7,500 | | 42,188 | 6,662 | | | (19,736) | | 180,321 | 166,507 | 60,769 | 286,059 |
| 2009 | 56 | 22,478 | 7,500 | | 43,876 | 6,662 | | | (20,599) | | 174,188 | 173,168 | 58,968 | 288,387 |
| 2010 | 57 | 23,378 | | | 38,131 | 6,662 | (7,500) | | (21,415) | | 166,708 | 180,094 | 57,024 | 289,779 |
| 2011 | 58 | 24,313 | | | 39,656 | 6,662 | | | (22,005) | | 158,040 | 187,298 | 54,924 | 290,415 |
| 2012 | 59 | 25,285 | | | 41,242 | 6,662 | | | (22,619) | | 148,064 | 194,790 | 52,655 | 290,199 |
| 2013 | 60 | 26,297 | | | 42,892 | 6,662 | | | (23,257) | | 137,652 | 202,582 | 50,206 | 290,028 |
| 2014 | 61 | 27,349 | | | 44,608 | 6,662 | | | (23,921) | | 124,742 | 210,685 | 47,560 | 287,867 |
| 2015 | 62 | 28,442 | | | 46,392 | 6,662 | | | (24,612) | | 100,130 | 219,112 | 44,703 | 274,539 |
| 2016 | 63 | 29,580 | | | 48,248 | 6,662 | | | (25,330) | | 74,800 | 227,877 | 41,617 | 261,060 |

Ron and Nancy's Scenario 1–A Graph

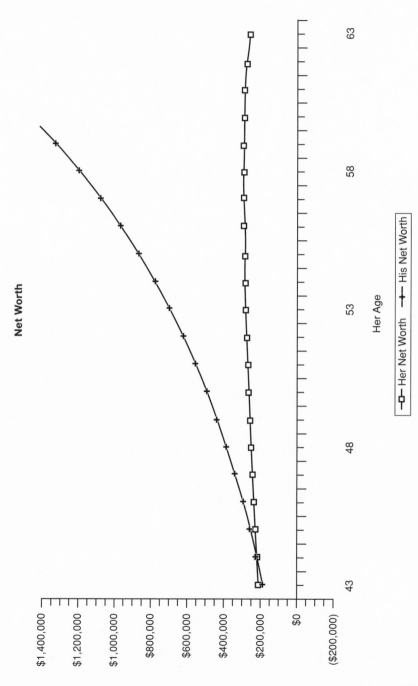

**Net Worth**

Her Age

—□— Her Net Worth   —+— His Net Worth

Copyright 1987–1996 Quantum Financial, Inc.

# TABLE 6-5

## Nancy's Spreadsheet (Scenario 2)

| Year 1996 | Age 43 | Income Take-Home Pay 4.0% $13,500 | Child Support 11 $11,600 | Maint. Support 5 $15,000 | Expenses Living Expenses 4.0% $35,676 | Real Estate Payments 30 $555 | Other Expenses | Taxes on Maint. | Annual Net Cash Flow | Working Capital 5.0% $5,000 | Retirement Accounts 8.0% $172,975 | Fair Market Value Real Estate 4.0% $100,000 | Real Estate Mortgage 30 8.0% $75,000 | Net Worth |
|---|---|---|---|---|---|---|---|---|---|---|---|---|---|---|
| 1996 | 43 | $13,500 | $11,600 | $15,000 | $29,014 | $6,662 | | $1,645 | $ 2,779 | $ 8,029 | $186,813 | $104,000 | $74,338 | $224,504 |
| 1997 | 44 | 14,040 | 11,600 | 15,000 | 30,175 | 6,662 | | 1,645 | 2,158 | 10,589 | 201,758 | 108,160 | 73,623 | 246,884 |
| 1988 | 45 | 14,602 | 11,600 | 15,000 | 31,382 | 6,662 | | 1,645 | 1,513 | 12,631 | 217,899 | 112,486 | 72,851 | 270,166 |
| 1999 | 46 | 15,186 | 11,600 | 15,000 | 32,637 | 6,662 | | 1,645 | 842 | 14,105 | 235,331 | 116,986 | 72,017 | 294,404 |
| 2000 | 47 | 15,793 | 11,600 | 15,000 | 33,942 | 6,662 | | 1,645 | 144 | 14,954 | 254,157 | 121,665 | 71,116 | 319,660 |
| 2001 | 48 | 16,425 | 11,600 | 12,000 | 35,300 | 6,662 | | 1,045 | (2,982) | 12,719 | 274,490 | 126,532 | 70,143 | 343,597 |
| 2002 | 49 | 17,082 | 11,600 | 12,000 | 36,712 | 6,662 | | 1,045 | (3,737) | 9,618 | 296,449 | 131,593 | 69,093 | 368,567 |
| 2003 | 50 | 17,765 | 11,600 | 12,000 | 38,180 | 6,662 | | 1,045 | (4,522) | 5,576 | 320,165 | 136,857 | 67,958 | 394,640 |
| 2004 | 51 | 18,476 | 11,600 | 12,000 | 39,708 | 6,662 | | 1,045 | (5,339) | 516 | 345,778 | 142,331 | 66,733 | 421,892 |
| 2005 | 52 | 19,215 | 11,600 | 12,000 | 41,296 | 6,662 | | 1,045 | (6,188) | | 364,076 | 148,024 | 65,409 | 446,691 |
| 2006 | 53 | 19,983 | 11,600 | 12,000 | 42,948 | 6,662 | | 1,045 | (19,072) | | 361,574 | 153,945 | 63,980 | 451,540 |
| 2007 | 54 | 20,783 | 7,500 | | 40,566 | 6,662 | ($4,100) | | (18,945) | | 359,082 | 160,103 | 62,436 | 456,749 |
| 2008 | 55 | 21,614 | 7,500 | | 42,188 | 6,662 | | | (19,736) | | 355,078 | 166,507 | 60,769 | 460,817 |
| 2009 | 56 | 22,478 | 7,500 | | 43,876 | 6,662 | | | (20,599) | | 349,389 | 173,168 | 58,968 | 463,588 |
| 2010 | 57 | 23,378 | | | 38,131 | 6,662 | (7,500) | | (21,415) | | 341,826 | 180,094 | 57,024 | 464,896 |
| 2011 | 58 | 24,313 | | | 39,656 | 6,662 | | | (22,005) | | 332,678 | 187,298 | 54,924 | 465,053 |
| 2012 | 59 | 25,285 | | | 41,242 | 6,662 | | | (22,619) | | 321,781 | 194,790 | 52,655 | 463,916 |
| 2013 | 60 | 26,297 | | | 42,892 | 6,662 | | | (23,257) | | 312,811 | 202,582 | 50,206 | 465,187 |
| 2014 | 61 | 27,349 | | | 44,608 | 6,662 | | | (23,921) | | 302,311 | 210,685 | 47,560 | 465,257 |
| 2015 | 62 | 28,442 | | | 46,392 | 6,662 | | | (24,612) | | 289,570 | 219,112 | 44,703 | 463,979 |
| 2016 | 63 | 29,580 | | | 48,248 | 6,662 | | | (25,330) | | 274,930 | 227,877 | 41,617 | 461,189 |

106

# Ron's Spreadsheet (Scenario 2)

| Year | Age | Income Take-Home Pay 4.0% | Retire at 65 | Expenses Living Expenses 4.0% | Real Estate Payments 26 | Other Expenses | Child Support | Maint. Support | Annual Net Cash Flow | Working Capital 5.0% | Retirement Accounts 8.0% | Fair Market Value Real Estate 4.0% | Real Estate Mortgage 26 10.3% | Net Worth |
|---|---|---|---|---|---|---|---|---|---|---|---|---|---|---|
| 1996 | 43 | $51,098 | $39,924 | $25,980 | $720 | | $11,600 | $10,050 | | $11,750 | $123,525 | $105,000 | $77,300 | |
| 1996 | 43 | $51,098 | | $17,343 | $8,637 | | $11,600 | $10,050 | $3,468 | $15,805 | $133,407 | $109,200 | $76,625 | $181,788 |
| 1997 | 44 | 53,142 | | 18,037 | 8,637 | | 11,600 | 10,050 | 4,818 | 21,414 | 144,080 | 113,568 | 75,880 | 203,181 |
| 1998 | 45 | 55,268 | | 18,758 | 8,637 | | 11,600 | 10,050 | 6,222 | 28,707 | 155,606 | 118,111 | 75,059 | 227,365 |
| 1999 | 46 | 57,478 | | 19,509 | 8,637 | | 11,600 | 10,050 | 7,683 | 37,825 | 168,054 | 122,835 | 74,153 | 254,562 |
| 2000 | 47 | 59,777 | | 20,289 | 8,637 | | 11,600 | 10,050 | 9,202 | 48,918 | 181,499 | 127,749 | 73,153 | 285,012 |
| 2001 | 48 | 62,169 | | 21,100 | 8,637 | | 11,600 | 8,040 | 12,791 | 64,155 | 196,019 | 132,858 | 72,051 | 320,981 |
| 2002 | 49 | 64,655 | | 21,944 | 8,637 | | 11,600 | 8,040 | 14,434 | 81,796 | 211,700 | 138,173 | 70,835 | 360,834 |
| 2003 | 50 | 67,241 | | 22,822 | 8,637 | | 11,600 | 8,040 | 16,142 | 102,028 | 228,636 | 143,700 | 69,494 | 404,870 |
| 2004 | 51 | 69,931 | | 23,735 | 8,637 | | 11,600 | 8,040 | 17,919 | 125,049 | 246,927 | 149,448 | 68,015 | 453,408 |
| 2005 | 52 | 72,728 | | 24,684 | 8,367 | | 11,600 | 8,040 | 19,767 | 151,068 | 266,681 | 155,426 | 66,384 | 506,791 |
| 2006 | 53 | 75,638 | | 25,672 | 8,637 | | 11,600 | 8,040 | 29,729 | 188,350 | 288,016 | 161,643 | 64,584 | 573,424 |
| 2007 | 54 | 78,663 | | 26,699 | 8,637 | | 7,500 | | 35,827 | 233,595 | 311,057 | 168,108 | 62,599 | 650,161 |
| 2008 | 55 | 81,810 | | 27,767 | 8,367 | | 7,500 | | 37,906 | 283,180 | 335,942 | 174,833 | 60,410 | 733,544 |
| 2009 | 56 | 85,082 | | 28,877 | 8,637 | | 7,500 | | 40,068 | 337,407 | 362,817 | 181,826 | 57,995 | 824,054 |
| 2010 | 57 | 88,485 | | 30,032 | 8,637 | | | | 49,816 | 404,093 | 391,842 | 189,099 | 55,332 | 929,702 |
| 2011 | 58 | 92,025 | | 31,234 | 8,637 | | | | 52,154 | 476,451 | 423,190 | 196,663 | 52,394 | 1,043,910 |
| 2012 | 59 | 95,706 | | 32,483 | 8,637 | | | | 54,585 | 554,859 | 457,045 | 204,530 | 49,153 | 1,167,280 |
| 2013 | 60 | 99,534 | | 33,782 | 8,637 | | | | 57,114 | 639,716 | 493,608 | 212,711 | 45,579 | 1,300,456 |
| 2014 | 61 | 103,515 | | 35,134 | 8,637 | | | | 59,744 | 731,447 | 533,097 | 221,219 | 41,637 | 1,444,126 |
| 2015 | 62 | 107,656 | | 36,539 | 8,637 | | | | 62,480 | 830,499 | 575,745 | 230,068 | 37,288 | 1,599,023 |
| 2016 | 63 | 111,962 | | 38,001 | 8,637 | | | | 65,324 | 937,348 | 621,804 | 239,271 | 32,492 | 1,765,931 |

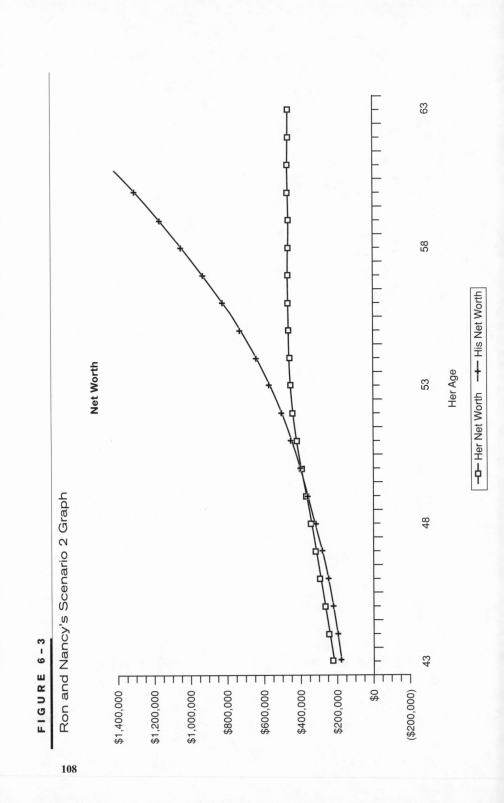

**FIGURE 6 - 3**

Ron and Nancy's Scenario 2 Graph

**Net Worth**

# Financial Affidavit

## THE IMPORTANCE OF THE FINANCIAL AFFIDAVIT

Gloria was getting divorced from a highly paid executive. She had not filled out an affidavit when she came to my office for her first appointment. I asked how much she spent each month. She replied that she had no idea—she just wrote checks. I asked where the money came from. She said that her husband put the money into the checking account and she just wrote the checks. I then asked how much he put into the checking account and Gloria replied, "I don't know. I don't even know how much he earns. I just know that it's a lot. All I know is that I write checks for whatever I want and there is always enough in the account to cover it."

In Gloria's case, we went back through months of check registers and credit card statements to produce a spreadsheet of expenses. It was very time-consuming but necessary. You will come across hundreds of Glorias in your practice. This chapter will guide you through the areas I have identified as essential in reporting income and expenses by both husband and wife.

Every state has some kind of form that the divorcing parties fill in, which then becomes part of the court record. This form shows income from all sources, deductions from their paychecks, living expenses, debt, and assets. Each party swears that the information on his or her form is accurate.

These forms, called *financial affidavits,* provide the basis for our financial projections. And even though they are sworn to be true, it is amazing how often they change! And the changes always seem to entail an increase in expenses.

# How to Find Errors

After having seen 500 to 600 of these affidavits, I have come to some conclusions as to average spending habits and where the errors are most commonly made.

For an example of this, let's look at Sara and Bob's financial affidavits. We will be looking at a standard affidavit used in the state of Colorado. Sara and Bob have been married 12 years and have one child. Figure 7–1 represents Sara's income and expense pages.

## Sara's Income

There are numerous errors and adjustments on Sara's forms. On the income page, note

1. Line 3: Sara is paid $440 every other week. She thinks that by doubling each number, she will reflect monthly totals. In fact, she needs to multiply each number by 26 and divide by 12 to get her monthly figures.
2. Line 4: Her corrected gross is $953, not $880.
3. Line 5: Her corrected federal income tax is increased to $70.
4. Her corrected Social Security payment is $73.
5. Her corrected state income tax is $23.
6. Her corrected total deductions are $166.
7. Line 6: Her corrected net income is $787.
8. Line 7: "other sources of income" includes other jobs, retirement income, dividend income that is actually paid out, bonuses, and so on.

## Sara's Expenses

Sara's expenses also needed adjustments.

9. Line 14 C (grocery store items): The average seems to be $150 to $200 per person per month. Under $150 per person seems to be low and over $200 is on the high side unless they entertain.

Entertaining will push the average up, especially if liquor is served. Teenagers also keep the grocery bill on the high side. Women usually have higher grocery bills than men.

10. Line 14 C (restaurant meals): Men tend to spend more than women on eating out.

11. Line 14 D (medical): If medical costs are reimbursed by the insurance company, most people tend to forget how much is received. These categories are for unreimbursed expenses only!

12. Line 14 D (other): In 90 percent of the cases, "other medical" involves therapy. It seems that everyone going through divorce is in therapy!

13. Line 14 E: Under health insurance, a lot of mistakes are made. Typically, the wife puts zero because she is not making an insurance payment. Or she will say, "Well, I am going to get COBRA, but I do not know how much it is." You or she can call the benefits department of the husband's company and ask how much the COBRA payment is.

14. Line 14 F (transportation): What if her car is paid for and she shows no payment? Talk to the attorney on the case and think about entering an estimated payment for a future car. (This is especially applicable when the car is 10 or more years old.) Maintenance includes tires, license plates, oil changes, and repairs.

15. Line 14 G (clothing): Her clothing costs are on the low side for herself and her teenage son. The average is in the range of $100 to 200 per person per month.

16. Line 14 L (miscellaneous): Some large expenses fall under "miscellaneous." They include gifts (Christmas, birthdays, weddings), donations, magazines, books, newspapers, cable TV, pets, hobbies, personal care (such as haircuts), and lawn service.

17. Line 15 (debts): Under "Debts," do not put the house mortgage or car loan. They have already been included in the "housing" (A) and "transportation" (F) sections. This section is used for credit cards, other bank loans, lines of credit, or anything that they owe anybody else.

**FIGURE 7-1**

Financial Affidavit

Name ___Sara Anderson_____

1. Occupation ___Secretary_____

2. Primary employer's name _____
   Hours worked per week _____40_____

3. I am paid ☐ weekly ☒ every other week ☐ twice each month ☐ montly
   Amount of each check (gross) _____ 440

4. Monthly gross income _____ ~~880~~ 953

5. Monthly payroll deductions
   (Number of exemptions being claimed:_____)
   Federal income tax _____66._____ 70
   Social Security _____61._____ 73
   State income tax _____21._____ 23
   Health insurance premium _____
   Life insurance premium _____
   Credit union _____
   401(k) _____
            Total deductions from this employment: _____ 155. 166

6. Net monthly take-home pay from primary employer _____ 721. 787

7. Ohter sources and amounts of income
        SOURCE                          AMOUNT
   _____          _____
   _____          _____

8. Deductions from other income sources listed in part 7
        DEDUCTIONS                      AMOUNT
   _____          _____
   _____          _____

9. Net monthly income from other sources _____

10. NET MONTHLY INCOME from ALL sources _____

11. Net monthly income of children _____

12. Income reported on last federal return _____

13. Monthly gross income of other party _____
    Monthly net income of other party _____

                                                      (continued)

14.  MONTHLY EXPENSES for ___/___ adult and ___/___ children:

TOTAL

A.  HOUSING
   Rent/first mortgage _____620_____
   Second mortgage_____
   Homeowner's fee _____          620
B.  UTILITIES
   Gas and electric _____100_____
   Telephone _____50_____
   Water and sewer _____
   Trash collection _____          150
C.  FOOD
   Grocery store items _____400_____   ⑨
   Restaurant meals _____15_____   ⑩          415
D.  MEDICAL (after insurance)
   Doctor _____25_____   ⑪
   Dentist _____30_____
   Prescriptions _____20_____
   Other _____   ⑫          15
E.  INSURANCE
   Life insurance _____50_____   ⑬
   Health Insurance _____175_____
   Homeowner's _____25_____          250
F.  TRANSPORTATION
   Vehicle payment _____200_____   ⑭
   Fuel _____50_____
   Repair & maintenance ___65_____
   Insurance _____50_____
   Parking _____   ⑮          365
G.  CLOTHING                                                        150
H.  LAUNDRY                                                          _____
I.  CHILD CARE (and related)
   Child care _____
   Allowance _____          _____
J.  EDUCATION (and related)
   For children
      Tuition, books, & fees _____
      Lunches _____
   For spouse
      Tuition, books, & fees _____          _____
K.  RECREATION                                   ⑯                   250
L.  MISCELLANEOUS                                                   325
M.  TOTAL REQUIRED MONTHLY EXPENSES                                2,660

15.  DEBTS

| Creditor | Unpaid Balance | Monthly Payment ⑰ |
|---|---|---|
| A. _____ | $ _____ | $ _____ |
| B. _____ | $ _____ | $ _____ |
| C. _____ | $ _____ | $ _____ |
| D. _____ | $ _____ | $ _____ |
| E. _____ | $ _____ | $ _____ |

## Bob's Income

Now turn to Figure 7–2 for Bob's income page. He earned a gross income of $8,167 per month.

**1.** Line 5 (monthly payroll deductions): His Social Security deduction shows an obvious error because he is in a high tax bracket. His Social Security is taken out at the front of the year so he is putting down that whole payment and he is not averaging it over the year. The average deduction would be $372. It has been reduced, increasing his cash flow by $251 per month.

**2.** Line 5: Check out his income taxes. He has $1,910 for federal tax when it should be $1,696 and he has $385 for state tax when it should be $335. Another $264 has been found. It is not unusual to see federal taxes increase on a husband's affidavit when he knows he will be divorced by the next April. By that time, a refund is claimed. Money is being stashed.

**3.** Line 5 (credit union): Always ask the question, "What is this for?" In this case, Bob was saving $200 per month in his credit union. His car payment was $250; he had obtained the loan through the credit union. But check Figure 7–2 under F (transportation), and you will notice the same $250 under "vehicle payment." Bob is double-entering his car payment. The entire $450 payment comes back into additional cash flow.

**4.** Line 5 (401(k)): It's the same with the 401(k). The court allows you to put voluntary contributions to retirement plans back into cash flow. The reasoning is that the family needs the money before the savings account does.

**5.** Line 5 (total deductions from this employment): Corrected total deductions are $2,403.

**6.** Line 6 (net monthly take-home pay from primary employer): The corrected net take-home pay is $5,764.

## Bob's Expenses

Figure 7–2 lists Bob's expenses.

**7.** Line 14 A (housing): If the husband has moved out, he may be renting a room from a friend at a low rate. This is not likely to continue and this expense can be expected to go up.

**8.** Line 14 C (food): His expense for food is lower than it would be if he were eating out a lot, which is typical for a husband. If you find his grocery expense at $400 to $500 per month for one person, ask if he cooks or entertains a lot. If the answer is no, he is probably padding his account.

**9.** Line 14 K (recreation): Bob's recreation spending is high because he is dating again, which is expensive.

As you see by reviewing Sara and Bob's affidavits, it is important to know exactly how much the clients are spending and what their spending patterns are. Otherwise it is impossible to determine what their needs are and how to best meet those needs.

Chapter 15 ("Forms and Information Needed") has a more complete sample of a financial affidavit which will be helpful to you in gathering information.

**FIGURE 7-2**

Financial Affidavit

Name _Bob Anderson_

1. Occupation _Manager_

2. Primary employer's name _____
   Hours worked per week _____

3. I am paid ☐ weekly ☐ every other week ☐ twice each month ☒ montly
   Amount of each check (gross) _____

4. Monthly gross income                                            _8,167_

5. Monthly payroll deductions
   (Number of exemptions being claimed _____)
   Federal income tax _____ _1,916_     1,696 ②
   Social Security _____ _625_     372 ①
   State income tax _____ _385_     335 ②
   Health insurance premium _____
   Life insurance premium _____
   Credit union _____ _450_     0     ③
   401(k) _____ _400_     0     ④
              Total deductions from this employment: _____ ~~3,768~~ 2,403

6. Net monthly take-home pay from primary employer _____ ~~4,399~~ 5,764

7. Other sources and amounts of income
              SOURCE                              AMOUNT
       _____              _____
       _____              _____

8. Deductions from other income sources listed in part 7
              DEDUCTIONS                          AMOUNT
       _____              _____
       _____              _____

9. Net monthly income from other sources _____

10. NET MONTHLY INCOME from ALL sources _____

11. Net monthly income of children _____

12. Income reported on last federal return _____

13. Monthly gross income of other party _____
    Monthly net income of other party _____

                                                                    (continued)

14. MONTHLY EXPENSES for ___/___ adult and ___0___ children:

                                                                          TOTAL

  A. HOUSING
      Rent/first mortgage _____500_____ ⑦
      Second mortgage_____
      Homeowner's fee _____     500

  B. UTILITIES
      Gas and electric _____100_____
      Telephone _____50_____
      Water and sewer _____
      Trash collection _____     150

  C. FOOD
      Grocery store items _____175_____ ⑧
      Restaurant meals _____220_____     395

  D. MEDICAL (after insurance)
      Doctor _____
      Dentist _____30_____
      Prescriptons _____
      Other _____     30

  E. INSURANCE
      Life insurance _____80_____
      Health insurance _____
      Homeowner's _____25_____     105

  F. TRANSPORTATION
      Vehicle payment _____250_____
      Fuel _____100_____
      Repair & maintenance __100__
      Insurance _____80_____
      Parking _____     530

  G. CLOTHING     100

  H. LAUNDRY _____

  I. CHILD CARE (and related)
      Child care _____
      Allowance _____ _____

  J. EDUCATION (and related)
      For children
          Tuition, books, & fees _____
          Lunches _____
      For spouse
          Tuition, books, & fees _____

  K. RECREATION                 ⑨     400

  L. MISCELLANEOUS     300

  M. TOTAL REQUIRED MONTHLY EXPENSES _____ 2,510

15. DEBTS

| | Creditor | Unpaid Balance | Monthly Payment |
|---|---|---|---|
| A. | _____ | $ _____ | $ _____ |
| B. | _____ | $ _____ | $ _____ |
| C. | _____ | $ _____ | $ _____ |
| D. | _____ | $ _____ | $ _____ |
| E. | _____ | $ _____ | $ _____ |

# Maintenance (Alimony)

For all practical purposes, alimony and maintenance mean the same thing. The two words are used interchangeably. Simply put, alimony is a series of payments from one spouse to the other, or to a third party on behalf of the receiving spouse. In most cases, the wife is the recipient; in some, the husband receives it. Alimony is taxable income to the person who receives it and, with few exceptions, it is tax-deductible by the person who pays it. (This chapter's section "Tax Issues of Maintenance" covers exceptions.)

Sometimes in a long-term marriage (one of more than 10 years), either the wife has not worked outside the home or she has stayed home with the children until they are in school or have left home. Both of these positions limit her ability to build a career. She and her husband may have decided as a couple that she would be responsible for running the household and/or caring for the children.

In most cases, if she did hold a job, her income was less than her husband's—sometimes substantially lower. If a transfer or move was indicated, the decision would be based on his job and career. If they moved, she would usually have to quit her job and start over somewhere else.

Career decisions and divorce can negatively affect the husband as well. If the wife's career is more lucrative, the husband may have refused a job transfer so that his wife could pursue her career. He could be stuck in a dead-end position that he couldn't leave without jeopardizing his pension.

When you are "fired" from the job of husband or wife, no one offers you an unemployment check. Is it any wonder, then, that alimony often becomes a major battleground in divorce?

Deciding whether a spouse should receive alimony (and, if so, how much) is based on certain criteria. Some state statutes give detailed criteria. In addition, the spouse might be awarded rehabilitative maintenance, or the terms might state that the payments be modifiable or nonmodifiable. Of course, as with any source of income, there are tax laws you need to be aware of, including front loading of maintenance options, life insurance treatments, and exceptions to recapture rules.

## CRITERIA FOR RECEIVING MAINTENANCE

It used to be that "fault" determined alimony. Today, alimony is awarded based on any of the following criteria: need, ability to pay, length of marriage, previous lifestyle, and the age and health of both parties.

## Need

The criterion of need asks the basic question, "Does the recipient have enough money to live on?" This would include income from earning ability, earnings from property received in the property division, and earnings from separate property. Alimony may be necessary to prevent the wife (and sometimes the husband) from becoming dependent upon welfare.

Minor children are also considered when evaluating need. Although child support is a separate issue, the mother (if she is the custodial parent) must be able to care adequately for the children. That means a roof over the kids' heads, food on the table, and utilities to heat, light, and provide water in their home.

Even though a spouse may think an alimony award is needed, the court sometimes finds otherwise. Take this example. Sophia wanted maintenance from her husband. However, she had a trust set aside that was separate property; in that trust was over $1 million. The court deemed that she did not need maintenance because she had property that would provide income to her.

## Ability to Pay

The criterion of ability to pay takes into account whether the payor can afford to pay what is needed and still have enough to live on or to support a lifestyle roughly equivalent to his or her previous lifestyle.

An angry wife may say, "I want $6,000 a month," which is the husband's entire salary. The wife is acting out of anger, which is not unusual. It is your responsibility to get her to be more reasonable and realistic.

## Length of Marriage

A two-year marriage may not qualify for alimony, but a 25-year marriage probably will. A rule of thumb that is often used is that alimony may be awarded for half the number of years married.

## Previous Lifestyle

Previous lifestyle is a criterion that takes into account how the spouses are accustomed to living. In a 23-year marriage where the husband earns over $500,000 per year, he probably won't be able to justify that his wife only needs $50,000 per year in alimony. In contrast, neither member of a young couple who didn't earn much money should expect to become wealthy as a result of the divorce.

## Age and Health of Both Parties

The age and health of both parties is the final criterion when deciding maintenance. Issues may include

- Is he or she disabled?
- Is he already retired? If so, does he have guaranteed permanent income?
- If she is 60 years old and has never worked, it will be very difficult for her to find employment. She may need permanent maintenance.
- If she is in poor mental and/or physical health, she may not be able to find adequate employment.

### TERMS OF MAINTENANCE

Maintenance stops upon the death of the payor. Ways to guarantee maintenance are discussed later in this chapter. Maintenance usually ends upon the remarriage of the recipient. The section "Modifiable versus Nonmodifiable Maintenance" gives exceptions.

## REHABILITATIVE MAINTENANCE

In the 1970s, courts began to recognize the need for a transition period. It was unrealistic to think that the wife (or husband when the wife was the breadwinner) could instantly earn what her husband did, if ever. With that awakening, rehabilitative maintenance was birthed.

If the wife, for example, needs three years of school to finish her degree or time to update old skills, she may get *rehabilitative mainte-nance*. This will give her the temporary financial help that she needs until she can earn an amount sufficient to support herself.

In discussing rehabilitative maintenance with your clients, it's important to be realistic on your and your client's parts. Why? Sometimes a normal three-year degree becomes impossible while caring for three kids. Realistically, five years may be more in line. It shouldn't be viewed as an entitlement—to be stretched until every drop is taken. Rather, it can be a bridge from one "career" to the next.

## MODIFIABLE VERSUS
## NONMODIFIABLE MAINTENANCE

The one constant in life is change. Given that, it doesn't make much sense to assume that the final settlement decided in court will apply to all future scenarios. For example, one spouse may become unemployed; the other may become ill. Change can be positive too. One of the spouses may land a job that creates lucrative stock options and incentives; one could inherit a substantial sum of money, win a lawsuit, or even win the lottery. This type of windfall could lead to a decrease in maintenance.

To allow some flexibility to accommodate these potential changes, the court where the divorce is granted often maintains "jurisdiction" over the case. This allows any order of support to be modified when a change of circumstances makes it reasonable to do so. These changes in circumstances include increases or decreases in the income or expenses of either or both spouses, especially when such changes were outside the control of the individual.

What if the ex-wife gets a roommate who pays all the expenses? The husband's attorney could use this fact to request a reduction in his current alimony payment. Many states presume that when a spouse who receives maintenance moves in with another person, he or she need less monetary support.

After the divorce is final and an order of support is given, either spouse can go back into court and ask for a modification, either up or down. However, you and your client need to be aware that the judge may deny the request for modification. Not only that, but he or she may even rule in the opposite direction! So, before you go back to court to ask for a modification, be sure to examine the position and the soundness of the evidence.

Nonmodifiable maintenance is not used very often because it is a challenge to both sides, but there are certain advantages to it in some cases. Let's say that the divorce decree says that he is going to pay six years of maintenance nonmodifiable. This means that even if she gets married in two years, she still gets four more years of maintenance. While this appears to be a great deal for the recipient, it can work against her. What if she becomes disabled or otherwise needs more income? She cannot get more. At six years, all payments stop. Legally, she has no way to continue the maintenance income.

Many times, after maintenance is set up, the husband retires early. He won't want to pay maintenance anymore. To change the original orders, he'll have to go back to court and have them changed by a new court order. This means money is spent—both parties will have to hire attorneys to get it changed. Even if they both agree, they have to draw up a new agreement. They each should be represented by an attorney.

Most often, the case will end up in court. Rarely does the wife want to reduce the maintenance amount. Or perhaps he wants to drop it totally, while she is receptive to some decrease but not a decrease to zero. If they cannot agree on what number should be used, they end up in front of a judge.

## TAX ISSUES OF MAINTENANCE

To be considered maintenance, the payments must meet all of the following requirements:

1. All payments must be made in cash, check, or money order
2. There must be a written court order or separation agreement.
3. The couple may not agree that the payments are not to receive alimony tax treatment.
4. The couple may not be residing in the same household.
5. The payments must terminate upon the payor's death.

**6.** The exspouses may not file a joint tax return.

**7.** No portion of the payment may be considered child support.[1]

Let's look at each requirement in more detail.

**1.** All payments must be made in cash, check, or money order.

To qualify as alimony, payments made from one spouse to the other must be made in cash or the equivalent of cash. Transfers of services or property do not qualify as alimony. However, it is possible for payments made to a third party on behalf of his or her spouse to qualify as alimony.

Under the terms of their divorce decree, Stanley is required to pay his ex-wife Marilyn $5,000 per year for the next five years. Six months after the decree is entered, Marilyn decides to return to school to qualify for a better-paying job. She calls Stanley and asks him to pay her $5,000 tuition instead of sending her the monthly alimony checks. Stanley agrees and on September 4, 1994, pays $2,500 for Marilyn's first-semester tuition. For Stanley to deduct this payment as alimony, he must obtain a written statement from Marilyn indicating that they agreed that his payment of the tuition was alimony. This written statement must be received before Stanley files his original (not an amended) income tax return for 1994.

As tax return time approaches, Stanley is eager to get his tax refund. On February 14, he files his 1994 return without waiting for the written statement from Marilyn. On March 1, he receives the statement from Marilyn. He may not deduct the payments as alimony because he failed to get the required written statement before the return was filed.[2]

Here's another example. Under the terms of their separation agreement, Robert must pay the mortgage, real estate taxes, and insurance premiums on a home owned solely by his exwife, Julia. Robert may deduct these payments as alimony. Julia must include the payments in her income, but she is entitled to claim deductions for the amount of the real estate taxes and mortgage interest if she itemizes her deductions.[3]

Payments made to maintain property owned by the payor-spouse may not qualify as alimony. Assume the same facts from above, except that Robert and Julia own the residence as joint tenants. Since he has a 50 percent ownership interest in the home, Robert may deduct only half of the payments as alimony. However, he is entitled to claim deductions for

---

1. *Divorce and Taxes* (Chicago: Commerce Clearing House, 1992), p. 11.
2. Ibid. p. 16.
3. Ibid. p. 15.

interest with respect to his own half of the mortgage payments. Similarly, Julia must report half of the payments and income and can only claim half of the deductible interest.[4]

**2.** There must be a written court order or separation agreement.

There must be a written separation agreement or court order in order for the payments to qualify as alimony.

As an example, Craig and Sally are separated. Craig sends Sally a letter offering to pay her $400 a month alimony for three years. Sally feels this is a slap in the face since she raised his kids and kept his house clean for 18 years. She does not respond. Craig starts sending the $400 per month. Sally cashes the checks. Since there is no written agreement, he may not deduct the payments as alimony.

Here's another example. According to their divorce decree, Allen is to send Marian $750 per month alimony for 10 years. Two years after their divorce, Marian loses her job and prevails on Allen's good nature to increase her alimony for six months until she gets started in a new job. He starts sending her an extra $200 per month. This was an oral agreement, not written. No postdecree modification was made so he may not deduct the additional amounts.

**3.** The couple may not agree that the payments are not to receive alimony tax treatment.

The divorcing couple must not opt out of alimony treatment for federal income tax purposes. Maintenance is taxable to the person who receives it. It's tax-deductible by the person who pays it.

**4.** The divorcing couple may not be members of the same household at the time payment is made after the final decree.

Sometimes a couple gets divorced but neither can afford to move. They reach an agreement: She lives upstairs and he lives downstairs. He pays her maintenance—as specified in the decree—but he cannot deduct it on his tax return. Since they live in the same house, it is not considered maintenance.

**5.** The obligation to make payments must terminate upon the spouse's death.

The obligation ceases upon the death of the payor or the payee.

---

4. Ibid. p. 16.

**6.** The exspouses may not file a joint tax return.

Many couples file for the year they got divorced. This is an error. The filing status is the status they have on December 31 of the year they are filing. If they are divorced during 1994, on December 31, 1994, they are not married so they may not file a joint return.

**7.** If any portion of the payment is considered to be child support, then that portion cannot be treated as alimony.

During the temporary separation agreement and until the divorce is final, the couple can decide whether the alimony payments should be considered taxable or nontaxable. Many times, any money paid to the spouse up to the time of permanent orders is not considered maintenance. On the other hand, sometimes the temporary orders can consider it to be maintenance so it is taxable. Written agreements and good communication are essential here. Nothing should ever be assumed by either party or attorney.

## FRONT-LOADING OF MAINTENANCE

The IRS has a rule that says that if the payor of alimony wants to deduct everything over $15,000 per year, payments must last for at least three years. The recapture rules were designed to prevent nondeductible property settlement payments from being deducted as alimony. The rules come into effect to the extent that alimony payments decrease annually in excess of $15,000 during the first three calendar years.

To the extent that the payor spouse has paid "excess alimony," the excess alimony is to be recaptured in the payor spouse's taxable income beginning in the third year after divorce. The payee spouse is entitled to deduct the recaptured amount from gross income in the third year after divorce.

For example, Trish tells her husband Robert that after their divorce, she plans to go back to school for one year and finish her degree. Then she will be able to get a certain job that, after a year, will pay her $30,000 a year and she will no longer need alimony. She asks Robert if he will support her for those two years. He agrees. Her expenses for those two years, including school costs, are $60,000 the first year and $30,000 the second year.

A friend tells Robert about an IRS rule saying that if he wants to deduct everything over $15,000, alimony must go for at least three years, but the rule doesn't stipulate the amount he must pay. Robert wants to deduct the whole amount so he offers to pay Trish $1,000 the third year to satisfy the IRS ruling. Here's what it looks like:

> First year      $60,000
> Second year   30,000
> Third year        1,000

However, the friend didn't tell Robert about the second part of the IRS rule. Some friend! The IRS says that if the payments drop by more than $15,000 from one year to the next, there is tax recapture on the amount over $15,000. In Robert's case, the alimony dropped by $30,000 from year 1 to year 2, and by $29,000 from year 2 to year 3. Robert will have to pay tax recapture on $37,500. Let's see how it works.

The formulas for figuring front-loading of alimony (sometimes called *recapture of excess alimony*) include two steps:

**1.** The amount of excess payments in the second calendar year is the excess (if any) of the total alimony paid during the second year minus the sum of the amount of alimony paid in the third year plus $15,000.

$$\text{Excess payment} = \underset{\text{in second year}}{\text{Alimony paid}} - \underset{\text{in third year}}{\text{Alimony paid}} + \$15,000$$

**2.** The amount of excess payments in the first calendar year is the excess (if any) of the total alimony paid in the first year minus the sum of $15,000 and the average of the amount of alimony paid in the second year (less excess payments for that year) and the amount of alimony paid in the third year.

$$\underset{\text{payment}}{\text{Excess}} = \underset{\text{first year}}{\text{Alimony paid in}} - \$15,000 - \frac{\underset{\text{second year}}{\text{Alimony paid in}} - \underset{\text{second year}}{\text{Excess payments}} + \underset{\text{third year}}{\text{Alimony paid in}}}{2}$$

Let's put Robert's numbers into the formulas.

Step 1:

$$\text{Excess payment} = \$30,000 - (\$1,000 + \$15,000) = \$16,000$$

Step 2:

$$\text{Excess} = \$60,000 - \$15,000 - \frac{(\$30,000 - \$16,000 + \$1,000)}{2} = \$37,500$$

In one divorce case, the husband was to pay his ex-wife $650 a month for eight years. Immediately after the decree, he got a position out in San Jose, California, at one of the big computer companies. He was delighted with his moving bonus plus the large salary. Then it hit him. He did not want to be financially tied to his wife for eight years. He called his attorney and said, "I want to buy her out of maintenance. Figure out how much that is." They figured out that it was something like $46,000 and he sent her a check. The following April, he was not happy because he had to pay recapture tax. He got bad advice from his attorney and he paid for it. In this case, a financial expert could have helped him.

## EXCEPTIONS TO RECAPTURE RULES

The recapture rules do not apply if:

1. Either spouse dies before the end of the third postseparation year or the spouse entitled to receive the payments remarries before the end of the third postseparation year.
2. The amount of payments fluctuates for reasons not in control of the payor spouse. For example, the payments might be a fixed percentage of income from a business or property, or from compensation for employment or self-employment.

Let's say Bert agrees to pay Maggie 25 percent of the net income from his farm each year for a period of three years. In the first year, the net income from the farm is $120,000 and Bert sends Maggie a check for $40,000. During the second year, the area is hit by severe weather and most of his crops are wiped out. That year, the farm's net income is only $32,000 so Bert sends Maggie a check for $8,000. In the third year, the farming business suffers a loss of $10,000 so Bert makes no payment to Maggie that year. In this case, no recapture is required.

## DECLINING MAINTENANCE

Keeping in mind the front-loading of maintenance rules, there are some advantages to structuring maintenance that decreases from year to year. For example, Lucy and Brian structured their divorce settlement so that Lucy would receive payments over a six-year period. She would receive $2,000 per month for two years, while she was finishing her physical therapist degree. After completing her degree, she would get $1,500 per month for two years, while she was getting her business set up. During the final two years, she would get $1,000 per month. At the completion of six years, all payments would stop.

Lucy liked this arrangement because the gradual decline gave her a chance to get used to it and prepare to adjust her standard of living. In addition, she could tell how much she would need to work to replace the lost income.

Brian liked this arrangement because he could see and feel the decline of maintenance. And, he knew it wasn't going to go on forever. This is an important factor for the majority of individuals who are required to pay maintenance. They want a light at the end of the tunnel.

## GUARANTEEING MAINTENANCE

Even though the divorce decree stipulates that one spouse is to pay the other a certain amount of maintenance for a certain period of time, it doesn't prove that it will happen. There are several ways an exspouse can get out of making the payments. Fortunately, there are also several ways to guard against this and guarantee that payments will be made. These ways include life insurance, disability insurance, and annuities.

## Life Insurance

Alimony payments stop upon the death of the payor. Therefore, it should be stipulated in the divorce decree that life insurance will be carried on the life of the payor to replace alimony in the event of the payor's death.

If a new policy is to be purchased, it should be done before the divorce is final. For instance, Alex agreed to buy a life insurance policy to ensure his alimony payments to Sarah. After the divorce was final, he applied for the insurance and took his health exam. He was found to be uninsurable. If Sarah had known this before the divorce, her attorney would have asked for a different settlement. It was now too late.

The recipient spouse should either own the life insurance or be an irrevocable beneficiary for two reasons:

**1.** *To ensure payment of premiums.* For example, Bernie was ordered by the court to carry a $50,000 life insurance policy on his life payable to Betty in the event of his death. A few years later, Bernie got tired of making the insurance payments and canceled the life insurance policy. No one was aware that he did this. When Bernie died, there was no insurance to cover Betty's alimony.

2. *Tax treatment.* If the beneficiary spouse either owns the policy or is an irrevocable beneficiary, and the premium payments are made under a legal obligation imposed by the divorce decree, the premiums are considered to be alimony (tax-deductible by the payor and taxable to the recipient).

Chapter 10 says more about life insurance.

## Disability Insurance

A second way to guarantee the stream of maintenance income is to have disability insurance on the payor's ability to earn income. Assume, for example, that a husband is to pay his ex-wife $1,200 per month based on his salary of $6,000 per month. Then he becomes disabled. If he had disability insurance, he might then receive $4,000 per month tax-free and could continue making maintenance payments. If he had no insurance and no income, he would probably go back to court and ask to have maintenance modified.

The ex-wife cannot own the disability policy, but she may make the payments on it so that she knows it stays in force. She will also, in that case, be notified of any changes made in the policy.

## Annuity

A third way to guarantee maintenance is to have the payor buy an annuity that pays an amount per month that equals the maintenance payment.

Assume that Ted buys a $200,000 annuity that will pay out $850 per month (the agreed-upon maintenance payment) in interest only. If the payment represents interest-only payments, they are taxable to him as income, but deductible by him as alimony. His wife Judy will pay taxes on the payments. This way, the payment is always made on time, the payor does not need to worry about it, the recipient does not have to worry about it, and the principal can still belong to the payor. At the end of the agreed-upon term of maintenance, Ted can stop the interest-only payments.

If the agreed-upon maintenance is $1,000 per month and Ted chooses to annuitize the annuity and receive $1,000 per month, part of the payment (say $850) will be taxable to him, but he will be able to deduct the whole $1,000 as alimony payments. At the end of the term of maintenance, he will continue to receive the $1,000 per month.

## CHAPTER 9

# Child Support

Every parent is obligated to support his or her children, regardless of divorce. In a divorce situation, the noncustodial parent is usually ordered to pay some child support to the custodial parent. The remainder of the child's expenses are paid by the custodial parent.

All states now have child support guidelines that help the courts decide the amount of child support to be paid. The support obligation of each parent is often based on the ratio of each parent's income, the percentage of time the child spends with each parent, and the amount of alimony paid to the custodial parent.

Here's an example. Paul's gross income is $4,300 a month and Becky's gross income is $900 a month; together they earn $5,200.

|  |  |  |
|---|---|---|
| Paul | $4,300 | 83% |
| Becky | 900 | 17% |
|  | $5,200 |  |

Paul is earning 83 percent of the total and Becky is earning 17 percent. They have two children. The Child Support Guidelines in Colorado for two children is $983 per month. Using these guidelines, take 83 percent of the suggested monthly payment of $983 and you will determine that Paul owes Becky $813 in monthly child support *if he pays no maintenance.*

But let's assume that he is going to pay her maintenance of $1,000 a month. At this point, you would then subtract the $1,000 from his income and add it to hers.

```
Paul    $4,300 − $1,000 = $3,300  63%
Becky      900 + $1,000 = $1,900  37%
        $5,200            $5,200
```

The totals stay the same but the percentages change. Now his percentage is 63 percent. Using the same guidelines formula, multiply $983 by 63 percent and you determine that Paul will pay $624 per month instead of $813.

You may be thinking, Why would Paul want to pay a total of $1,624 (i.e., $1,000 maintenance and $624 child support) when he could pay $813 in child support—with no maintenance? Unfor-

> The rule of thumb is as maintenance increases, child support decreases.

tunately, the amount of child support paid is often less than the actual amount required to meet the needs of growing children. And second, many times the child support is not paid at all.

Many times there is suspicion or anger from the husband. He thinks, "I am not sure that my ex-wife will spend the money on the children—she probably will spend it on herself!" Child support is based on income so, obviously, it is based on some kind of lifestyle that was already established.

The husband thinks, "If I want my children to live in this kind of a house, I have to pay enough child support that will make that kind of house payment. That means my ex-wife is going to be there, too."

So, many times, the husband will get angry because his ex-wife is getting maintenance on top of child support. Or, if she is not getting maintenance, he feels that she is living off the child support. However, there are many fathers who understand that for the children to live in the kind of house they're accustomed to, the wife has to be there with them.

Paul and Becky present a simplistic example. There are other factors that enter in, such as whether he is paying for child care, health insurance, and/or education or school expenses. These factors would make adjustments necessary to the child support amount. Also, if there are four children and three will live with the mother and one with the father, that would impact the financial picture. Another factor is the percentage of time he is going to have the children.

## MODIFYING CHILD SUPPORT

What happens when circumstances change after the divorce is final? Say, the husband loses his job, the wife loses her job, one person becomes disabled, a settlement or judgment is awarded that was started when still married, or one of them wins the lottery.

The property settlement is final and you usually cannot change anything about the property settlement unless you can determine fraud. However, the child support and maintenance can be modified unless there was agreement to the contrary. They are usually modified for a substantial change of circumstances. How much of a change constitutes a "substantial" change in circumstance? Obviously, if the income changes, that would change the child support according to the Child Support Guidelines.

There is an interesting issue. Assume there are two children and child support is agreed upon. At some point, the older child decides to go live with Dad in the summertime. Since he's paying the full cost of supporting this child at his house (at least for several months), Dad says, "Now I only have to pay half the child support," and he sends a check for half the amount. Because it was not changed by a court order, he still owes the whole amount and the ex-wife could force him to pay that back child support he did not pay.

Or, suppose that both kids go to live with Dad during the summer. Dad says, "I do not have to pay any child support during the summer since both kids are living with me," but the court order says that he must pay so much every month. It does not say "nine months out of the year." Unless it is in the court order, he is liable for those payments, and his ex-wife could sue him for that money. It is important to have written agreements as circumstances change.

## INCOME TAX CONSIDERATIONS

Child support payments cannot be deducted by the payor and are not includable in the income of the recipient.

If the divorcing parents have only one child, that child can be counted as an exemption by only one parent in a given year. Unless otherwise specified, the exemption usually goes to the parent who has physical custody of the child for the greater portion of the calendar year.

The exemption can be traded back and forth year to year between the parents with a written waiver or IRS Form 8332. Once the custodial parent has executed the waiver, the noncustodial parent must attach the form to his or her income tax return. If the waiver is for more than one year, a copy of the form must be attached to the noncustodial parent's return for each year.

If the family has more than one child, the parents may divide up the exemptions. The children's Social Security numbers must be listed on each parent's tax return. IMPORTANT: If both parents claim the same child or children on their tax return, they are inviting an IRS audit.

For either parent to claim the exemption, the child must be in custody of at least one parent for more than half of the calendar year. If the child lives with a grandparent or someone other than a parent for more than half of the calendar year, neither parent can claim the exemption.

## CHILD CARE CREDIT

A custodial parent who pays child care expenses so that he or she can be gainfully employed may be eligible for a tax credit for up to $2,400 ($4,800 for two or more children) of those expenses. To claim this credit, the parent must maintain a household that is the home of at least one child, and the day care expenses must be paid to someone who is not claimed as a dependent.

Only the custodial parent is entitled to claim both the child and the dependent care credit. This is true even if the custodial parent does not claim the dependency exemption for the child. A noncustodial parent may not claim a child care credit for expenses incurred even if that parent is entitled to claim the exemption for the child.

Here's an example. Carl and Mandy's son Bret, age 4, lives with Mandy four days a week and with Carl three days a week. Both Carl and Mandy work outside the home and each pays half of the $5,000 per year that it costs to have Bret in day care during the work week. Mandy is entitled to claim a child care credit for her share of the day care expenses. Although Carl and Mandy each have custody of Bret for a significant portion of the week, Mandy is considered the custodial parent because Bret spends a greater percentage of time with her than he does with Carl.

## HEAD OF HOUSEHOLD

A head-of-household filing status is available for those who are divorced (single), who provide more than half the cost of maintaining the household, and whose household is the principal home of at least one qualifying person for more than half of the year. A *qualifying person* is their child or any other person who qualifies as their dependent.

In determining whether the home is the principal home of the child for more than half of the year, do not count absences for vacation, sickness, or school as time spent away from home if it was reasonable to assume that the child would return to the home.

## CONTINGENCIES: SIX-MONTH RULE

If the separation agreement specifies a certain amount for "family support" instead of clearly stating a specific amount for child support and a specific amount for alimony, there could be adverse tax consequences.

If the family support is reduced within six months before or after the child reaches the age of majority, and is reduced by the amount that the parents had allocated for child support, the entire amount of the reduction could be deemed child support and nondeductible as alimony. This will be retroactive to the date of the first payment, and any deductions for these payments as alimony will be retroactively disallowed.

## CHAPTER 10

# Insurance

**B**ack in Chapter 4, you read about career assets that need to be considered as dividable property. There are two more that you need to know about: health insurance and life insurance.

## HEALTH INSURANCE AND COBRA

In the traditional marriage where the husband is the main wage earner, one concern is maintaining health insurance for the ex-wife after divorce. It is not uncommon for women over 40 years of age to develop severe health problems. Some become almost uninsurable, at least at a reasonable cost. This is a real concern where, all of a sudden, they are on their own and responsible for acquiring health insurance.

The Older Women's League (OWL) worked hard to get the Consolidated Omnibus Budget Reconciliation Act (COBRA) law passed in 1986. It allows women to continue to get health insurance from their ex-husband's company (if it has at least 20 employees), for three years after the divorce. The normal COBRA provision states that, if an employee is fired or leaves a job, he or she can get health insurance from that company for 18 months. However, in a divorce, it is extended to three years or 36 months.

Assume that Sara from Chapter 7 ("Financial Affidavit") decides to continue health insurance under COBRA. Sara must pay the premium as agreed. If she misses a premium payment, the health insurance company can drop her and they do not need to reinstate her. So she must pay that premium on time. Typically, Sara will not get the discounted group rate but will be charged the full rate. It is important to shop for health insurance. Even though the COBRA provision may supply a quick solution to health care coverage, it may not be the best. It may be purchased at a lesser cost somewhere else.

Talk to your female clients about health insurance. A client (healthy or not) could say, "I am going to be covered by COBRA from Bob's work." Tell her about clients who develop health problems.

Encourage clients over 40 to explore other options. Tell them, "I would advise that you shop for health insurance because if you can match the rate from Bob's company or get a lower premium with another company, you should buy your own. Then if something happens, as long as you pay your premiums, you are covered. Otherwise, at the end of three years, COBRA drops you, and then you have to start shopping for your own insurance. By that time, you might be uninsurable and not able to find insurance."

Most states have insurance for those who are uninsurable and cannot get health insurance any other way. As may be expected, this insurance is very costly. It is better to look ahead and get your client individual health insurance for a lower premium while she's still healthy than to gamble that your client will still be healthy three years later.

Is health insurance a marital asset? Some companies provide health benefits for employees after they retire. Some lawyers are starting to consider this an asset since the Financial Accounting Standards Board in 1993 began requiring employers to calculate the present value of the future benefits and show a liability for that value in their financial reports.

> If the benefits are a liability to the employer, there's a good argument they should also be an asset to the employee.

## LIFE INSURANCE

Since maintenance stops upon the death of the payor, the stream of payments should be covered by life insurance on the life of the payor. This should be part of the final divorce settlement.

I always recommend that the wife own the life insurance policy and make the premium payments. This prevents any changes in the policy without her knowledge.

Here's an example. Joan was receiving $400 per month in alimony from her ex-husband Jerry. The court had ordered Jerry to carry life insurance on his life payable to Joan as long as alimony was being paid. After three years, Jerry was tired of making the insurance payments so he stopped and the insurance was canceled. Nobody knew about it until one year later when Jerry was in a car accident and died two weeks later of complications from his injuries. Alimony came to an abrupt halt and there was no life insurance! Yes, Jerry was in contempt of court but it didn't make any difference now.

I also recommend that, if the wife can afford it, the life insurance build cash value. Then, the cash account within the policy is hers to do with as she wishes. She may even use it for retirement. She can borrow from it at any time, or cancel the policy and use the cash.

Another option would be to purchase level term insurance for the life of maintenance. She could "buy term and invest the difference" in a mutual fund that she can watch.

A third recommendation is to make sure that, if new insurance is needed, it be applied for before the divorce is final. Then, if he cannot pass the physical and cannot get new insurance, there is still time to modify the final settlement to make up for this surprise.

If the court orders the husband to purchase insurance to cover maintenance and/or child support, those premium payments are treated like alimony for tax purposes and he can deduct them from his taxable income. Likewise, the wife will need to declare them as taxable income.

Is term insurance ever considered a marital asset? Yes. If the insured has since become uninsurable, it could be considered an asset. Remember this.

## CHAPTER 11

# Social Security

$\mathbf{F}$or all the examples in this chapter, we will assume that the wife was the lower-earning spouse. In real life, the husband could be the lower-earning spouse, in which case all rules would apply to him.

You probably know that the wife is entitled to half the ex-husband's Social Security provided certain provisions are met:

1. The husband is entitled to receive Social Security benefits,
2. They had been married for 10 years before the divorce became final,
3. The wife is not married,
4. The wife is age 62 or over, and
5. The wife is not entitled to a retirement benefit that equals or exceeds half the husband's benefit.

Since this rule does not diminish the amount the husband receives at retirement, he usually doesn't worry about this.

A wife who is age 62 or over and who has been divorced for at least two years will be able to receive benefits based on the earnings of a former husband regardless of whether the former husband has retired or applied for benefits.

If the wife of a retired or disabled worker is caring for the worker's under-age-16 or disabled child, the monthly benefit equals half of the worker's benefit regardless of his age. If the wife is not caring for a child, monthly benefits equal half of the husband's, but if the wife chooses to start receiving benefits at age 62, the benefit that she would receive at age 65 is reduced by 25 percent. If the wife chooses to receive the reduced benefit at age 62, she is not entitled to the full benefit upon reaching age 65.

Assume the husband will get $750 a month when he retires. If they have been married 10 years or longer, she could get $375 (half of the husband's benefit) at age 65.

Husband   $750
Wife       $375

What if he gets remarried? If he is married to his second wife for 10 years and they get divorced, wife 2 gets $375, wife 1 gets $375, and he still gets $750. It does not matter how many wives he has. As long as he is married to each one for 10 years or longer, they each get half of his Social Security benefit.

Husband   $750
Wife 1     $375
Wife 2     $375

One reason why Social Security is in so much financial trouble is that the fund is covering and paying for items that it was not originally designed to do, such as former spouses.

What if the wife gets remarried? If she is married at retirement time, she looks to her current husband for her benefit. But if she has been married to husband 1 for 10 years and they get divorced, she is entitled to half of husband 1's benefits or half of husband 2 benefits. She has a choice.

Husband 1   $750     Husband 2   $600
Wife         $375     Wife         $300

If husband 2 is entitled to $600 at retirement, she obviously will choose the benefits from husband 1. They are more.

Assume she begins working after the kids are raised and by the time she retires, she can get $450 from her own Social Security account. Now she has the choice at retirement time of taking $450 from her own account, $300 from husband 2's account, or $375 from husband 1's account. She can only have one—hers, his, or his. Obviously, she would take her own account, which would pay her $450 per month.

What if they get divorced and he dies? The wife is entitled to full widow's benefits (100 percent of the deceased husband's benefits) if

1. The deceased husband was entitled to Social Security benefits,
2. They had been married for 10 years before the divorce became final,
3. The widow is age 60 or over, or is between ages 50 and 60 and disabled,
4. The widow is not married, and
5. The widow is not entitled to a retirement benefit that is equal to or greater than the deceased husband's benefit.

Wife 2 also gets full widow's benefits if she meets the above five requirements.

A widow's remarriage after age 60 *will not prevent* her from being entitled to widow's benefits on her prior deceased husband's earnings. A widow's remarriage before age 60 *will prevent* entitlement to widow's benefits unless the subsequent marriage ends, whether by death, divorce, or annulment. If the subsequent marriage ends, the widow may become entitled or reentitled to benefits on the prior deceased spouse's earnings beginning with the month the subsequent marriage ends.

As an example, assume that Maude's first husband died. At age 58, she met a wonderful widower and wanted to remarry but she realized that she would lose her entitlement to all of the deceased spouse's Social Security benefits when she turned age 60. This may explain why many senior citizens are living together unmarried.

Social Security benefits payable to the ex-wife are reduced by government retirement payments to the husband. These payments are based on his own earnings in employment not covered by Social Security on the last day of such employment. The reduction is two-thirds of the pension. Thus, the wife's benefit is reduced $2 for every $3 of the government pension.

## CHAPTER 12

# Debt, Credit, and Bankruptcy

## DEBT

As you saw in Chapter 4, property is classified as marital and separate. The same classifications apply to debt. In general, both parties are responsible for any debts incurred during the marriage—it does not matter who really spent the money. When the property is divided up during the divorce, the person who gets the asset usually also gets the responsibility for any loans against that asset.

It's in your client's best interests to pay off as many debts as possible before or at the time of the final decree. To do so, clients could use liquid assets such as bank accounts, stocks, and bonds. It may make sense to sell assets to accumulate some extra cash. The most easily sold assets include extra cars, vacation homes, and excess furniture.

If your clients can't pay off the debts, then the decree must state who will pay which debt and within what period of time.

There are generally four types of debt to consider: secured debt, unsecured debt, tax debt, and divorce expense debt.

### Secured Debt

Secured debt includes the mortgage on the home or other real estate, as well as loans on cars, trucks, and other vehicles. It should be made very clear in the separation agreement who will pay which debt. If one spouse fails to make a payment on a debt that is secured by an asset, the creditor can pursue the other spouse.

## Unsecured Debt

Unsecured debt includes credit cards, personal bank loans, lines of credit, and loans from parents and friends. These debts may be divided equitably. The court also considers who is better able to pay the debt.

For unsecured debt, the separation agreement needs to include a *hold harmless clause.* This will indemnify the nonpaying spouse, which means that the paying spouse gives the nonpaying spouse the right to collect not only all missed payments, but also damages, interest, and attorneys' fees if payments were not made. Without a hold harmless clause, the nonpaying spouse has the right to collect only the missed payments.

Financial advisors, lawyers, and clients all need to be aware that even though something is agreed to and included in the divorce decree, it doesn't mean that it will happen as planned. Often the legal decision and the financial outcome are very different things.

Here's an example: Tracy and Paul were married for eight years, during which time Tracy ran her credit cards to the limit with her compulsive spending. The court held Tracy solely responsible for paying the $12,000 in credit card debt. After the divorce, however, Tracy didn't change her ways and was unable to pay off her debt. The credit card companies came after Paul, who ended up paying them off. One solution would have been to pay off the credit cards with assets at the time of divorce or for Paul to have received more property to offset this possibility.

## Tax Debt

Just because the divorce settlement is final doesn't mean the parties are exempt from possible future tax debt. For three years after the divorce, the IRS can perform a random audit of the divorced parties' joint tax return. In addition, the IRS can question a joint return—if it has good cause to do so—for seven years. It can also audit a return whenever it feels fraud is involved. To avoid potential tax costs, the divorce agreement should have provisions that spell out what happens if any additional interest, penalties, or taxes are found, as well as where the money comes from to pay for an audit.

## Divorce Expense Debt

Although it isn't always clear who is liable for debts incurred during the separation, typically these debts are the responsibility of the person who incurred them. An exception would be if the wife runs up debt to buy food, clothing, shelter, or medical care for the children. The husband is probably obliged to pay those expenses if the wife cannot.

At times, one or the other party may have paid some divorce expenses before the divorce process was officially started. Remind your clients that they may want to get credit for these in the agreement.

Your clients will accrue other costs during the divorce process, including fees for court filings, appraisals, mediation, and attorneys. Other less obvious expenses are accounting, financial planning, and counseling. The separation agreement needs language that states who is responsible for these expenses.

There are also divorce expenses that may accrue after the decree, such as attorney fees for doing QDROs and title transfers. Other such postdecree expenses are tax preparation fees for the final joint tax return, mediation fees, and long-term divorce counseling for the parents or the children. Who pays? Spell it out clearly so there are no disputes at a later date.

## CREDIT

A creditor cannot close an account just because the account holder's marital status has changed. An exception would be if there is a proven inability or unwillingness to pay. However, the creditor can require a new application if the original application was based on only the other spouse's financial statement. The creditor must allow use of the account while the new application is being reviewed.

If the spouses hold charge accounts jointly, they will have the same credit history. If one spouse merely used the accounts as a signee, it may be necessary to confirm the fact that he or she was equally responsible for the payments. This can be done with proof of canceled checks and a financial statement that shows that spouse's ability to pay.

If your client has a good credit history and the necessary income, he or she should have little or no problem opening new accounts in his or her name only. If, however, the client was the spouse who was unemployed during the marriage and never had a credit card in his or her name, he or she may need a cosigner.

Your client may still be responsible for joint accounts even after the divorce is final. You should see to it that prior to the final decree, all joint accounts are paid off and closed, and that new accounts are started in the individual's names.

Also warn your clients about running up charge account bills as part of divorce planning or retaliation. If it can later be proven that these expenditures were not agreed upon jointly (or they were not for necessities such as food, housing, clothing, or health care), they may not be considered joint debt.

> Creditors don't care how the separation agreement divides responsibility for debt. Each person is liable for the full amount of debt on joint cards until the bill is paid.

## BANKRUPTCY

The word *bankruptcy* strikes fear in the hearts of many people—especially those going through divorce. Many wives who are trying to decide whether it is better to ask for alimony or a property settlement note are caught in indecision. Perhaps the husband has threatened either to leave the country if he has to pay alimony or to declare bankruptcy if he has to pay a property settlement note. Let's look at some of the rules of bankruptcy as they apply in divorce situations.

There are two types of bankruptcy available: Chapter 13 (which allows you to develop a payoff plan over a three-year period) and Chapter 7 (which allows you to liquidate all of your assets and use the proceeds to pay off debts, erasing the debts that cannot be paid in full).

Chapter 7 bankruptcy forgives all unsecured debts, and requires the forfeiture of all assets over certain minimum protected amounts. Creditors have the right to repossess their fair share of the assets. The net proceeds from the sale of assets are divided pro rata among the creditors.

Chapter 13 bankruptcy may preserve the assets and allow the debtor to pay off all the secured debt as well as a portion of the unsecured debt, and discharge the rest of the unsecured debt. The debtor needs to make payments under a plan.

Here are some things to remember:

- (If a spouse files bankruptcy before, during, or after divorce, the creditors will seek out the other spouse for payment of marital debt—no matter what was agreed to in the separation agreement.

- While the couple is still married, they can file for bankruptcy jointly. This will eliminate all separate debts of the husband, separate debts of the wife, and jointly incurred marital debts.

Promissory notes or property settlement notes, especially unsecured notes, are almost always wiped out in bankruptcy. Some secured notes, depending on the property that secures them, can also be discharged.

As an example, say Sam and Trudy divided all their assets. However, to achieve a 50/50 division, Sam still owed Trudy $82,000. Sam signed a property settlement note to pay Trudy the $82,000 over a 10-year period at 7 percent interest. After the divorce, Sam filed for bankruptcy and listed the property settlement note as one of his debts. Trudy never received a penny of the money that was due her.

> Certain debts cannot be discharged in bankruptcy. These include child support, maintenance, some student loans, and recent taxes.

## Dividing Marital Property and Debts

Many people try to divide each asset as they discuss it ("Your half of the house is $4,000, my half of the house is $4,000"). Since you will rarely divide the house like this, this may not be the most useful way to go about it. It may be more practical, to begin with, to list each asset as a whole under the name of the person who will keep it. For example, in the wife's column, list the marital equity in the house if she is thinking of continuing to live there. List the entire value of the husband's retirement in his column if that is your initial inclination. An advantage to this method is that it allows you to see the balance, or lack of it, of your initial plan as you develop it.

If you want to know dollar values, you may need a third party, such as an appraiser, to help you determine them.

This is the time for your client to have a real heart-to-heart discussion with the exspouse to reveal the range of their sense of fairness. Ask

- Is the only possibility for them a 50/50 division of things by value? By number?
- Are they more interested in cash than in things?
- Will they take less than 50 percent if their share is all cash?
- Are they more interested in future security than in present assets?

- If they are willing to wait for a buyout of their share, such as house or retirement, are they looking for more than 50 percent to compensate them for waiting?
- Are they interested in a lopsided agreement (more going to one than to the other) to compensate for the larger earnings of one of them now?
- Do they want to be "made whole" (end up where they were at the beginning of the relationship)?
- Do they need to be compensated "off the top" for some contribution they made to the acquisition of property?
- Is there a possibility that any assets/investments are hidden?

If you can get them to agree on a generic plan that meets both person's ideas of fairness, you will find you have an agreement that practically writes itself.

As you allocate the debts, decide first whether they are marital, separate, or a mix. Then agree who will pay off the balance of each. Remember that the problem of unsecured debts may be more easily handled as a budget item than as division of property.

Think beyond the short term to the long-term effect of the division of assets and debts you are considering. For example, suppose one spouse gets all assets that appreciate slowly or depreciate and that take money to maintain (home, car, furniture). Then suppose the other spouse takes all assets which increase in value or produce income (stock, retirement accounts, rental home). In such a case, even a few years after the divorce, what in the short term appeared to be a fair or equal division will look quite different. The net worth of the second spouse will far exceed the net worth of the first—and the gap will just continue to widen. It becomes your responsibility as a financial professional to consider this information before you decide what is really fair or equal in your client's situation.

## CHAPTER 13

# Mediation

No doubt, you have heard stories about lawyers who fan the flames to keep the adversarial atmosphere going. Care needs to be taken that couples who want to work out a settlement with a minimum of stress don't get caught up in the knock-off of *The War of the Roses* starring Michael Douglas, Kathleen Turner, and Danny DeVito. Unfortunately, once the flames have been fanned, the only person who will ever win is the attorney. The war of Justin and Stacy illustrates just that.

## THE WAR OF JUSTIN AND STACY

Justin and Stacy Smith had decided to call it quits after six years of marriage. They had no children. Justin had a new girlfriend and was feeling very guilty. He was a highly paid executive and offered to give Stacy almost everything: the house valued at $375,000, the $87,000 brokerage account, half his 401(k) which would give her $92,000, and $3,000 per month for three years. He also offered to pay the expenses for her to finish her master's degree in nursing. Before the breakup of the marriage, when they were on amiable terms, she estimated that she would earn $40,000-$50,000 per year with her master's degree in nursing.

Initially, Stacy was worried about his offering her everything. What was she missing? What was he hiding? Her friends kept telling her this was too good to be true. Instead of talking to Justin about a settlement, she hired the most expensive attorney she could find and paid him a large retainer to answer her questions. The attorney immediately filed a petition for divorce and initiated motions for protective orders and temporary maintenance.

Before Stacy had hired an attorney, the two of them had been communicating without legal counsel. When Justin called Stacy, she told him, "Have your attorney call my attorney." Since Justin had no attorney, he called Stacy's attorney and put forth his settlement offer again. The attorney stalled. He said he needed to do discovery and depositions. (He obviously needed to justify his fee.) Because he felt he was being put off, Justin again called Stacy and tried to settle, but she ignored him.

As time went by, he started feeling less guilty and more irritated. Justin hired his own attorney and paid another large retainer. Further negotiations for any type of settlement failed and the couple came to a standstill. What shouldn't have happened, happened. They prepared for a court trial.

Stacy's attorney asked for it all. He asked the court to give her the house, the entire brokerage account, half of the 401(k), $4,000 per month for four years, and $37,000 to pay her attorney's fees.

Justin's attorney said, "Whoa! Your honor, we need to present the facts. Initially my client offered to give Mrs. Smith the house, the brokerage account, half his 401(k), $3,000 per month maintenance for three years plus the amount she needed to finish graduate school. But the last few months for him have been hell. He has had to spend an exorbitant amount of money in legal fees and expert witness fees. His business has actually declined due to the attention he had to pay to attacks made by Mrs. Smith and her attorney. Granted, in my opinion, my client was overgenerous in his offer to her."

After hearing all the arguments, the judge was irritated. He chastised Stacy and her attorney for wasting the court's time. He gave Stacy $50,000 in cash, $500 per month maintenance for two years, and nothing extra for her attorney's fees. He gave Justin the house and his 401(k). The remainder of the brokerage account was long gone to pay attorneys' fees.

\*    \*    \*    \*

It is important for clients to get involved to bring sanity to a highly volatile and emotional environment. This is why mediation can work.

## WHAT IS MEDIATION?

This chapter is not meant to train the reader to be a mediator. Rather, it is to educate the reader about the process of mediation, what is involved, and some of the skills necessary to conduct successful mediation sessions with clients. Mediation is a relatively new process that is gaining recognition worldwide for its successful accomplishments. In our quest for divorce settlements instead of court trials in divorce, mediation is an important concept for us to be aware of.

This chapter would not be complete without mentioning the pioneer of divorce mediation, Gary J. Friedman, J.D. He realized in 1976 that there was a better way to resolve the issues surrounding divorce. Friedman shifted his focus "from doing battle, to helping people work together to make decisions regarding their lives rather than making one party a winner and the other a loser." He founded and directs the Center for Mediation in Law in Mill Valley, California. An internationally recognized authority on mediation, he has been training mediators and teaching mediation at Stanford Law School. His book, *A Guide to Divorce Mediation,* is considered essential reading for anyone interested in the subject.

Christine Coates, J.D., has been mediating divorce cases in Colorado since 1984. As a nationally known trainer and speaker on mediation she has an insider's view of what the process involves. She has the following to say about mediation.

### Christine:

What is mediation? Mediation is a process where a neutral person works with the divorcing parties to devise solutions that work for both of them. The mediator is a neutral, impartial person who doesn't take sides, has no interest in the outcome of the mediation, does not give or make decisions for the parties, and does not give legal advice. This is an important point. Even if an attorney is working as a mediator, it would be unethical for him or her—as the mediator—to give legal advice. However, the mediator can give legal *information.*

In the mediation process, the goal is to work with the parties and help them identify the issues. Together they uncover what each party really needs to have a fair settlement. To do that, all the facts are presented that are necessary to making an informed decision, and the mediator helps both parties resolve the issues to their satisfaction in a way that's fair to them.

Mediation is generally a voluntary process. The courts may order people to enter mediation, but the courts cannot order people to settle. Across the country, the courts are favoring mediation and ordering people to participate to make sure that they've had a chance to talk together before they end up in court.

The mediator's job is to be a facilitator and to help the couple work together. The mediator has no authority to force a decision upon them. Mediation is not therapy even though many mediators are therapists. It is not meant to work out what went wrong in their marriage, nor is it arbitration (where one person makes a decision for the couple). It is a very different method of resolving disputes.

In Colorado, mediation is generally confidential, which means that in most places, the mediator cannot be called into court to testify against either of the parties or to tell the court or the judge what has occurred in the mediation session. However, each state has its own rules on this issue. Mediation should be a safe forum where the couple can talk about proposed solutions with each other, resolve their disputes, and perhaps come up with a settlement.

The goal of mediation is to get past the positions that people come in with and work toward what they really need in order to be satisfied with an agreement and to walk out with a fair and satisfying agreement.

How does mediation work? There is a fairly predictable process. First of all, when two people visit the mediator, he or she gets to know them and spends some time telling them about mediation and how it works. The mediator asks them to sign a contract telling them what is expected from them and what they can expect from the mediator, and how the fees are charged.

Before beginning the mediation session in earnest, it is good to set ground rules. Two basic rules are (1) each person has the right to speak without being interrupted by the other and (2) neither spouse should put down the other or resort to name-calling.

The parties are told that the goal of mediation is to resolve their disputes, but the mediator is not going to do that for them. It is going to be their job and they are going to have to make their own decisions. The mediator will help them with what they need to know, what data they need to gather, and what information they need to bring to the table. He or she will help them figure out what to do and what agreements they need to reach. But the mediator is not going to reach decisions for them.

After meeting with them initially, some mediators meet with each person separately to get a sense of what each of them is feeling, what their fears are, and what's been going on with them that they may not feel comfortable talking about in front of the other. The mediator finds out what they really need to have happen to feel that they have had a fair agreement. However, some mediators never meet with the parties alone. That is just a different style.

After meeting with each alone, the three get back together to set the agenda. The mediator will have helped each of them to sort out the issues so they can decide which topics to talk about, such as property division, child support, and maintenance. Then they select an issue on which to begin working.

Sometimes, the mediator may decide with which issue to start. He or she may choose the issue that seems the easiest, especially if there is an issue on which they agree even though they may not have told each other. Choosing that issue will help them get a quick agreement right off the bat so they can reinforce their ability to continue to work together to make future agreements. However, sometimes they come in with issues that demand immediate attention. If they don't deal with them that first day, mediation may go nowhere. In those cases, the process may start with a tough issue.

After agreeing to the ground rules, they start the negotiating process. However, the couple often can't simply jump in and resolve issues. Many times, they first need to gather the information that is needed to make a decision. They need to know what their financial situation is, how much they spend, what the IRAs are worth, and so on. They will begin by filling out the standard financial affidavit form that is used in their state in compiling such information. Next they will list all the property. As a financial planner, you can help them gather all this information.

Once all the information is on the table, we can start generating options for settlement.

## THE NEGOTIATING PROCESS

After the ground rules are set and the couple has all their financial data in order, it is time to start the negotiating process. Michael Caplan, J.D., has been training mediators in Colorado since 1988 and is a mediator himself. He explains how a mediator typically approaches it.

### Michael:

There are basically two ways of negotiating or bargaining. The first method is *positional bargaining*. Positional bargaining starts with the solution. One party proposes a solution and the other makes an offer. There are counteroffers until, somewhere along the line, they hit on something that is successful and that works for both of them.

While this process sounds very calm and fair, there often is an undercurrent of selfishness. One client goes in with a low-ball offer and the other comes in with a high-ball offer. Somewhere in the middle, hopefully they will find a place where they are going to meet and where they think they are OK. Both people are also working from the notion that the "pie" is limited. They think, "There is only so much here and I have to get as much as I can. I am looking to win. And for me to win, you have to lose. My goal is to win as much as possible. For me to do that, you have to lose as much as possible."

Second, there is *interest-based bargaining*. It starts with parties educating each other about their interests. So instead of saying, "I must have this," they say, "I need this because this is what it will do for me."

It is based instead on "the pie is not limited, there is enough there for what we both want and need." Now that may not always be true, but that is the assumption that they start with. It is based on the premise that all our needs may not be met 100 percent in the way we most would like them to be, but they will be met in a way we can live with.

For example, when the wife says, "I need to have the house," the mediator shouldn't say, "You can't have the house if you can't afford it." What the mediator could say is, "Tell me more about why that is important to you." Then she might tell you, "Well, the house is the only liquid asset in which I have any money and it's the only asset I can get some money out of."

When the parties come in with their information, we often start getting information disagreements. I might say, "It looks like we need to determine the value of the house. What process do you want to use to determine what the value of that real estate is?" If they don't have a clear idea of what this means, I will suggest they get some help, such as from their own financial planner or other expert.

*    *    *    *

Christine Coates agrees with the importance of interest-based bargaining.

## Christine:
How do people negotiate? It means they turn from a position-based style to an interest-based style. A position is the specific proposal or solution

that a party adopts to meet his or her interests or needs. It is the party's solution to what he or she would really like to see happen. The person wants the other party to say yes or no.

This differs from the interest-based style, which is the concern or interest that the party wants to accomplish through his or her position. In almost every mediation, people come in with a position—they are very strong in what they want. But when the mediator starts probing, he or she finds that there is more than just that position. There is a need beneath it.

Say the wife states, "I must have $2,000 per month maintenance and that's final," or the husband says, "I'll pay $2,000 per month for five years. That's it. No more." Neither party can go very far with that. But when they start talking about what is beneath all that—is it for school, is it to meet reasonable needs, is it to support the household until the children are out of school?—there emerges room to negotiate.

> When anyone is stuck in a position, there is not a lot of room to negotiate.

## THE ROLE OF LISTENING IN MEDIATION

True, active listening is a big part of the mediator's job. According to Michael Caplan, "Effective listening is the other part of what we are doing." Here are some of his additional thoughts on listening.

### Michael:

Effective listening is the other part of what we are doing. How many times do we think we already know what the other person is trying to say? It takes energy to listen and you need to focus on the speaker. If I have my own talk going on in my head, I am going to have a hard time being able to hear. We need to check out what we think we heard to find out if we have it right and then we need to let the other party know that we really heard them.

So many times, women in the more traditional marriages have not really been heard. They really have not been listened to by their mate. The anger is there and sometimes it gets suppressed, so when it does come out it erupts like a volcano and involves issues that really may not be important.

Listening is different from problem solving or giving advice. How many times have you gone to a friend and started talking to him and he said, "Yeah, I had that problem once and this is what I did" or "You know, if you would only do this, that would settle it."

What I want to do when I am active listening is to feed back the feeling and content. "So you are really upset and a bit anxious about the fact that I came in late and you were worried about whether I was going to show up." Look for what the feeling is and give back the feeling first and try to match intensity.

*   *   *   *

Christine Coates agrees.

## Christine:

The mediator can never assume that he or she heard what the clients mean. For example, when women listen, many nod their head and say "Uh-huh, uh-huh." Men often just sit and listen, rarely showing any facial expression, much less head movement. When men hear a woman saying, "Uh-huh, uh-huh," they may think the woman is agreeing with them when the woman is actually only indicating that she is listening. When men sit and listen but don't say anything, women may think they aren't listening. This gender difference in listening styles leads to miscommunication.

Listening involves asking questions to make things more clear, but it is not interviewing. People want to know that they are being heard and then will get the facts afterward. *Listening is not problem solving*. It is not hearing what someone has to say and then jumping in with, "Here's what you need to do. I know exactly how you can fix this problem."

## Common Mistakes in Active Listening

- (Trying to solve the problem instead of focusing on what the other person is trying to say. Each person has the inherent ability to solve his or her own problems.
- (Telling the other person that you understand.
- Continuing to ask closed-end questions instead of open-ended questions.

## Active Listening Technique

When someone speaks, he or she is sending a message to the other person. They are sending it in a code. It has feelings and content. The listener's job is to decode what is being said. The listener has to feed back the message to make sure. Here's an example.

"It sounds like you're ___ (feeling) about ____ (content)."

"It sounds like you're really scared about what your husband's income will be."

"It sounds like you're really sad about having to move out of your house."

If you get it right, the person will respond, "Yeah, you've got it. That's right." If you get it wrong, the person will say, "No, that's not it."

Identify the feeling you are hearing, select the appropriate word that matches that feeling, and then match it in intensity. If someone says, "I am furious with him because he left me with no cash and no money in the bank," and you respond, "It sounds like you're a little miffed that there's no money in the bank account," that's not going to work because she's furious, she's not just a little miffed. You have to match the intensity as well.

---

**COMMUNICATION TIP: THE "MEDIATION TRIANGLE"**

When it comes to mediation, excellent listening skills are essential. Consider the "mediation triangle." The two clients and the mediator are sitting at a round table, equidistant apart. Let's say the wife tells the mediator her issues. The mediator reflects (states) back to her what was heard to make sure the underlying feeling is understood. The mediator then turns to the husband and repeats it to him in the new language.

This way, the wife has not voiced her frustration directly to him—which he has heard a dozen times already. Instead, she has channeled it through the mediator. Her husband now hears her frustration voiced in new terms. This may lead to a glimmer of understanding on his part. This can be a powerful technique in bringing couples to an acceptable level of agreement in any negotiation.

## Cindy and Bob: An Example of Active Listening in Mediation

Remember Bob and Cindy from Chapter 5? They're back and now they're meeting with a mediator. Here are some examples of good listening.

> *Cindy:* I *know* that he'll win in this divorce. He *always* gets his way.
>
> *Mediator:* It sounds like you're apprehensive about how this divorce is going to play out. It sounds like you're concerned that you're not going to get anything or be treated fairly.
>
> *Bob:* No matter what I've done, what I've given her, it's never enough.
>
> *Mediator:* It sounds like you're feeling unappreciated for what you've done in the marriage. It sounds like you're frustrated.
>
> *Cindy:* I've raised his kids while he worked the whole time. It's my turn now.
>
> *Mediator:* It sounds like you're feeling left out about not working during the marriage. It sounds like you feel cheated about raising kids and not working or getting paid.

When you start listening to what is behind the words and get to the feeling and content, then you start hearing what the client really needs. She's feeling trapped because she didn't get a chance to work. He's feeling unappreciated. Now you can look at an option that meets both of their needs.

## Listening Processes

In the following example, mediators Christine Coates and Michael Caplan take turns explaining each step in the process and describing what Cindy and Bob are experiencing.

### Christine:

If Cindy wants to keep the house and Bob wants to sell the house, they have to look at cash flow. Is she going to have enough cash to support this house? If not, where is it going to come from? If she gets the house, what will he get? Are we looking at a 50/50 property division or something different? The mediator will help them look at various options.

Often, the mediator will send them out to a financial planner or a CPA for an analysis of their financial situational. What are the ramifications of capital gains, basis, and so on? They need to put together a monthly cash flow statement so they know what it is going to cost each of them on a monthly basis to live. Is there income that can be shifted from one to the other?

It is wonderful when they come back with their spreadsheets. Now Cindy and Bob are ready to start talking. How are they going to make it work? We start generating their options.

We look at each agenda item. And, remember, we do it for interests, not positions. Cindy wants to keep the house. What is beneath that wish? Does the house really mean something to her? Is it so special because she put her heart and soul into it? Is it her dream house? Or is she afraid she will not be able to buy something else on her own because her income will be so low? Or is it because the kids need the stability of staying in the house? Talk about why she needs to stay in the house and then talk about that need and how it matches Bob's needs.

During the mediation process, I do a lot of active listening and ask a of open-ended questions. My job is not to interrogate the clients to get a long list of facts and data but to help them think through what's going on and what they need to have happen. One thing I don't do is cross-examine them.

## Michael:

Cindy says, "I want to stay in the home. I want the home." Bob comes back and says, "She cannot afford to stay in the home. It costs too damn much and I need some of that equity too." We can ask the next question, "Why is that important to you?"

Let us check it out a little bit. I'll ask, "So, Cindy, why is it so important for you to stay in the house?" She says, "Because it will be less upsetting to the children. They continue at their school and remain with their friends." I reply, "All right, so being in the same place and having continuity in school and stability in the home is important."

So now we frame it as how to create an environment for Cindy and the children that will give her and them the stability they need. Then we need to spend more time with what we mean by "stability."

I might start by asking questions to find out how long they need to stay in the home for stability and what that means. Do they need to be in the actual home or just the general neighborhood? Could they get a smaller home or an apartment in the neighborhood? Was this Cindy's family home? Does Cindy want the home because she spent time putting that place together and it was her basic emotional outlet?

# Reframing

## Christine:

Once we've listened and we've been able to figure out what they need, we can start reframing their needs that are interest-based instead of position-based. Cindy may see her situation as that she can't support herself without Bob's help. And for some reason, he won't give her the support. She may feel that Bob is selfish and only thinks about himself. She may see herself as unempowered. However, Bob may come in saying, "I worked really hard during our marriage and I'm willing to help her out for a while, but I'm not willing to go into poverty myself to support her extravagant lifestyle."

The mediator's task is to help them redefine the problem in ways that they can resolve it. We take the language they give us and *reframe* it. Cindy is talking about Bob's selfishness. Bob is talking about her extravagance. We need to pull those terms out of their statements and come up with something that makes sense for them.

## How to Do Reframing

**1.** Listen to what they have to say.

**2.** Pull out the toxic, destructive language.

**3.** Help them move from position to interest.

Here are some examples.

*Cindy:* I'm not going to be able to support my kids without Bob's help.

*Mediator:* I hear that you're really afraid that you're not going to be able to make it on your own without help from Bob.

*Cindy:* And what I really have to have is $3,000 a month maintenance for the next 10 years in order to get by.

The mediator restates this into interest behavior in terms of what she needs. What does she need? She needs to feel secure. She needs to feel that she can get through her college experience.

*Mediator:* It sounds like what you need is an agreement that gives you enough support to get through school and get your career on track. Is that right?

*Cindy:* Yeah.

So then you start talking about "How long will that be? What are you going to be doing during that time?"

Here's an example of working with people in reframing.

*Bob:* I worked hard to build my business. I did it single-handedly. There is no way I'm going to give any of it to her.

*Mediator:* Bob, what I hear you saying is that you want to be acknowledged for the work you put in to build your business. And you want to continue to run your business without Cindy's involvement. Is that what I hear you saying?

I turned what he was saying from "I'm not going to give her any of my business" to looking at (1) the acknowledgment he needs and (2) his not wanting her involved with his business.

Reframing is taking the "junk" out, listening to what they're saying, and trying to reframe or restate it in terms of their interests instead of their positions.

*Bob:* She can't have the rental house. She can't handle money and she won't be able to handle the rental. I'll probably have to pay the loan anyway when she defaults on it.

*Mediator:* It sounds like you're afraid that you'll end up paying this debt, that she will blow the money, and that you'll have to be more generous. You need to make sure that whatever financial arrangement you work out will be fair and you won't have to overpay.

*Cindy:* I'm not going to move out of the house. My lawyer says that the mother always gets the house and I need the house for the kids.

*Mediator:* It sounds like you're afraid the kids won't have a decent place to live. You want stability for the children.

*Bob:* We have to sell the house to pay off the debt. The monthly payment is too high. There is not enough money. She is going to bleed me dry. I'll walk away from my business before I'll give her more than three years of maintenance.

*Mediator:* It sounds like you are concerned about being poverty stricken after working so hard on your business. It sounds like what you need is an agreement that will reward you for working so hard in your business.

*Bob:* She is a competent person and can work just like me. I will give her a couple of years and then I'm not going to take care of her anymore.

*Mediator:* It sounds like you're concerned about being stuck with maintenance forever. One of your goals is that the settlement provides for Cindy to be self-sufficient in a few years.

*Cindy:* He's so selfish. He wants me to sell the house, which will hurt the kids. Doesn't he care about the kids?

*Mediator:* It sounds like you are afraid that the stability of the children living in that house and that neighborhood, and going to that school district, is going to be disrupted.

When we get the interests from each person, we can go to the problem-solving stage. Cindy's interest in the house is their children's stability. Bob's interest is to be debt-free and not have a cash flow problem. He wants maintenance to terminate in a reasonable length of time.

Try to frame a problem statement between the two of them. How can we handle the house? Combine their two interests into a joint problem statement.

*       *       *       *

## The Final Steps

Once they've gone through the whole agenda, the mediator will work with them to close the deal and pin it down. Throughout this process, the mediator will have advised them to be working with their separate attorneys, their financial planners, or their CPA to run options past them to make sure they're workable. When all the solutions are agreed upon, the mediator will fine-tune the agreement and draft it.

### WHERE TO FIND A MEDIATOR

When your client needs a mediator, who do you send them to? Being an attorney or therapist does not necessarily mean someone would make a good mediator. Unfortunately, few states have certification or a minimum amount of training necessary to become a mediator.

Mediators need special skills, especially in handling conflict. Before hiring a mediator, check out his or her qualifications. It's important to know who has had training and experience. Ask. The minimum amount of training acceptable is 40 hours.

There are mediation organizations in each state. Check the telephone book under "mediation" or call the American Academy of Family Mediators at 617-674-2663 in Lexington, Massachusetts. It can provide a list of mediators in your area.

## WHEN MEDIATION MAY NOT WORK

Some people feel that they are not candidates for mediation because they can't talk to each other, they can't communicate, or they're in high conflict. Well, almost everyone going through divorce is in that situation. It is known as the crazy time. People in divorce are often confused. They know how to push each other's buttons. It is the rare couple that can really communicate when they're going through divorce. The mediator is trained to deal with conflict.

Even so, there are some people who should not mediate. Often people going through divorce where there has been domestic violence should not be in mediation because there has been power imbalance in that relationship.

In situations where there is mental illness or substance abuse, mediation will probably not work. Substance abuse is an indication that at least one of the parties does not have the power to do what he or she needs to do. If they are addicted to a substance, the likelihood is that they also are unable to follow through on agreed-upon solutions.

Another area in which mediation should not be used is when one or both parties are ignoring the children's best interests.

In addition, if the clients want the mediator to make the decisions, or if one party seems to be giving in on all matters and you sense this was the norm in their relationship, these may not be good parties for mediation. Here's an example.

Norm and Donna came in to see the mediator. The one item that raised a red flag was the fact that Norm had done a lot of work in forming a software company. Because of his work and some contracts that he had put together, he had signed agreements that promised him bonuses for the next five years. Depending on profits, these agreements could give him up to $1 million per year for five years. Donna said that she had no right to those because they would come in after the divorce. She constantly looked at him for approval of what she was saying. The mediator asked Norm if he felt those were marital property and he guessed they were. The mediator then asked Donna again if she agreed that they were marital property. She looked timid and repeated that she wouldn't want to take those away from Norm. Finally, the mediator had to advise Donna to see an attorney before they could proceed further. She needed to know her legal rights.

## LEGAL SEPARATION

An option for some couples is a legal separation instead of a divorce. Under a legal separation, they divide their property and there may be child support and maintenance, but they are still legally married. A couple may choose this route for several reasons:

1. *Religious reasons.* Some religions frown on divorce. Many people are uncomfortable going against the teachings of their religion.

2. *Health insurance.* Even though COBRA allows the exspouse to retain health insurance for three years after the divorce is final, if the exspouse is uninsurable, insurance can be a great concern. A legal separation allows the person to remain on the working spouse's health insurance plan.

3. *Not wishing a divorce.* Many couples can't stand living together, but they also hate the thought of being divorced. A legal separation allows them to live their separate lives. And some spouses hold the secret thought that the marriage can be put back together. If the marriage turns out to be impossible to salvage, then a divorce can be filed and is easily accomplished as all the details, (such as dividing the property) have already been done.

## HIRING AN ATTORNEY

Some couples think they can hire one attorney and save costs. But the fact is, if they can't reach a settlement and have to go to court, each spouse will need his or her own attorney. While not illegal, one-lawyer divorces are ill-advised and can be considered unethical.

For example, issues may arise that neither party thought about but that must be resolved. It will be almost impossible for one attorney to help the couple resolve these issues if the solution is advantageous to one party and adverse to the other. In such a case, one spouse will have to hire another lawyer.

## CHAPTER 14

# If You Have to Go to Court

**W**e all hope for the best of all worlds: that we can settle our cases with both spouses feeling that they got a fair shake. If that doesn't happen, then we hope for the next best outcome: that we can reach an equitable settlement that preserves assets for our client.

Obviously, however, some cases aren't settled and they have to be decided in court. If there is even just one thing that cannot be agreed upon, the case will go to court for the judge to rule on that item only. Here is an example. As you'll see, sometimes it isn't worth your client's time and money to go through the process.

Ed and Sue had divided all their assets but one. Ed didn't want Sue to have any of his "poker savings account"—a $19,000 savings account representing his poker winnings over a 12-year period. Sue insisted that half of it was hers so Ed hired an expensive attorney and went to court rather than give in. He ended up spending $22,000 in fees—but he kept Sue from getting his savings account!

If a case you are working on does not settle, you could be called upon to appear as an expert witness in court on behalf of your client. If this happens, you want to be knowledgeable and prepared.

Helen Stone (a partner in Stone, Sheehy, Rosen & Byrne, P.C., in Boulder, Colorado) specializes in family law and bankruptcy. She lectures frequently on these topics. She has this to say about being an expert witness:

> Going to court does not make you an expert witness. What makes you an expert is your training as a CFP, the experience you have had analyzing

what people's incomes are, and doing calculations and predicting. It is your expertise that is helpful to this person going to court.

## PRELIMINARIES TO ACTING AS AN EXPERT WITNESS

What is an expert witness? A book that advises federal court juries gives the following definition:

> The rules of evidence ordinarily do not permit witnesses to testify as to opinions or conclusions. An exception to this rule exists as to those whom we call "expert witnesses." Witnesses who, by education and experience, have become expert in some art, science, profession, or calling, may state an opinion as to a relevant and material matter, in which they profess to be expert, and may also state their reasons for the opinion.[1]

Helen Stone explains this further.

### Helen:

The reason expert testimony is presented to a judge is to assist the trier of fact in determining and understanding specific evidence. The rules of evidence for lawyers provide for the use of expert testimony to do that. You are presented to the judge as an expert because you have specialized knowledge that will assist the judge in determining what the evidence is and how to sort through it. The rule says that if there is scientific, technical, or other specialized knowledge that will assist the trier of fact in understanding the evidence, then the lawyer can call an expert witness who has the requisite knowledge, skill or experience, training, and education to testify. That is the basis on which financial planners, certified public accountants, or lawyers are used as expert witnesses.

As a financial planner, you have some specialized knowledge that the judge lacks. Although the judge is going to be a person who has had legal training and has experienced a wide variety of cases, he or she is not likely to be a financial expert.

The judge may not have any background in the financial arena, or the judge may know some financial concepts but need a refresher in the subject area. You are valuable to the court because you have that expertise.

---

1. Devitt and Blackmar, *Federal Jury Practice and Instructions,* 3d ed., vol. 1 (West Publishing Company, 1977), § 15.22, p. 482.

The one thing that should give you some comfort when you first take the witness stand is that you know more about your subject matter than anybody in the courtroom. Even if you make a mistake, even if you are uncomfortable, and even if it is your first time in court, nobody there knows more about financial planning—especially what you have investigated and researched with respect to this case. Keeping that in mind will give you some comfort and some self-confidence because it is absolutely true. Your purpose in court is to communicate the information that you know to the judge.

$$* \quad * \quad * \quad *$$

Before actually presenting your report to the court and being questioned about it, some other things happen first. Your qualifications (or curriculum vitae) will be presented, you will be "qualified" as an expert witness, and there may be voir dire, which we'll discuss shortly.

## Your Curriculum Vitae

When you start working with an attorney, one of the first things that attorney is going to ask for is your curriculum vitae or resumé. He or she will want to see your credentials to determine if you can be an expert witness in court. The attorney cannot act as his or her own expert witness. The attorney has to hire outside experts and nobody else but you can show your work. You are the expert who produced the financial charts and graphs for your client. Now you are the one who has to answer the questions about them. Therefore, the attorney wants to know that you are going to qualify as an expert witness in court.

To be an expert witness, your curriculum vitae will list your qualifications that show you are an expert in financial issues of divorce. Start with your educational background and all the things that qualify you to be a financial planner. Your curriculum vitae should show

Current position.

Education and training.

Work history relating to financial planning.

Details of continuing education.

Publications including books and articles.

Workshop presentations, lectures, and teaching.

Honors and recognitions.

Expert witness experience.

Anything else related to being an expert in financial issues in divorce.

## Getting Qualified as an Expert Witness in Court

In court, you are sworn in by the judge or an assistant to the judge. After you repeat the oath, you sit in the chair for the expert witnesses. Then your client's attorney starts questioning you as to your qualifications. The attorney has not offered you as an expert yet. First, the attorney must show that you are qualified by questioning the information from your vitae. Finally, you will be offered to the court as an expert in financial planning.

## Voir Dire

After your client's attorney has offered you as an expert witness, the other attorney has a chance to do what is called *voir dire*. This means you will be asked questions designed to disqualify you and to show that you are not an expert. The goal of voir dire is to show that you are not qualified to talk about what you are talking about.

Barbara Stark is an attorney in private practice in New Haven, Connecticut. A fellow of the American Academy of Matrimonial Lawyers, she co-authored *Divorce Practice Handbook: Skills and Strategies for the Family Lawyer.* According to Ms. Stark, this is what to expect from voir dire.

### Barbara:

When an expert witness takes the stand and testifies to all of his or her qualifications, the other lawyer can get up and challenge you as an expert. This is known as voir dire. You'll be asked questions about your qualifications and experience, and those questions are designed to convince the court that you are not an expert.

Almost anybody who has training and experience above that of the normal lay person may be admitted as an expert witness. The reason that people go into your qualifications so much in both the direct examination and the voir dire is so the judge can have in his or her mind the degree of weight that should be given to your testimony.

There are four things you'll need to do on the witness stand.

1. Your first step is to explain the nature and the scope of your assignment. Every expert witness has an assignment. For instance, in this case, say your assignment from the attorney was to take certain property division, alimony, and child support scenarios and project their future economic consequences.
2. The second step is to explain how divorce planners use scenarios to show financial results of any given settlement. This mainly entails explaining methodology.
3. Next, summarize your work in the case—who you talked to, what information was assembled, what assumptions were made, and so on.
4. Last, admit your exhibits and explain your reports. Of course, before the trial, you will have coordinated with the attorney as to when the reports should be admitted.

*    *    *    *

After voir dire is complete and you have been qualified as an expert witness, you will go on to the next steps of the court process: direct examination and cross-examination.

## DIRECT EXAMINATION

As Barbara Stark says,

> The next step is direct examination. This is where your lawyer puts you on the stand. During direct examination, you are telling a story. Although your lawyer is asking you questions, he or she might as well not be there. You are the one on display. During direct examination, you are asked open-ended questions by your client's attorney. These are questions that cannot be answered yes or no, but rather need more complete responses. This gives you a chance to tell your story.

Typically, the direct examination of an expert witness is made up of three parts:

**1.** *Description of why the expert is qualified to render an opinion.* The purpose for getting you qualified is twofold: to get the opinion into evidence and to persuade the trier of fact (the judge) that your opinion is the correct one.

**2.** *Description of the nature and scope of the expert's assignment in this particular area.* You will be asked to describe the nature of your assignment to let the judge know why you are there and what you will be talking about. You will also be asked to describe the work you did to impress upon the judge that you were responsible and thorough.

**3.** *Description of the expert's conclusions and the information he or she has to support those conclusions.* You must make your testimony understandable and interesting. You must persuade the judge that your conclusions are fair and reasonable.

Barbara Stark, who has done countless cross-examinations, gives this example of direct examination. (You probably won't be asked about your breakfast in a real trial, but this dialogue gives you an idea of what to expect.)

*Attorney: (A)* What is your name?

*You: (Y)* Carol Ann Wilson.

*A:* Where are you staying here in Los Angeles?

*Y:* I am staying at the Sheraton.

*A:* Did you have breakfast there this morning?

*Y:* Yes, they have a wonderful breakfast buffet.

*A:* What did you have?

*Y:* I had fruit and toast and eggs with coffee.

*A:* Did you have any bacon with that?

*Y:* No, they didn't have any bacon on the buffet so I had one piece of sausage.

*A:* How much did you pay for your breakfast?

*Y:* The breakfast was included with the price of my room so I didn't pay anything this morning.

* * * *

Helen Stone gives this advice about the direct examination process.

## Helen:

During your direct examination, probably the most common objection that the other lawyer will raise is that what you are testifying to is hearsay. Remember that you are allowed to rely on hearsay. A vocational expert who may test a spouse's employability, is the kind of expert you have not talked to, but you are relying on the conclusions in the report, and that is permissible.

Be on the lookout for questions that ask you to give legal advice. It is OK for the lawyer to ask, "Is there enough money in this household to meet the necessary expenses?" because it only requests a simple cash flow analysis, which you do frequently in your business. On the other hand, asking the question, "Having looked at your chart and considered the expenses, is your client entitled to maintenance?" is calling for a legal conclusion. The lawyer will object and be sustained.

In direct examination, one area that comes up fairly regularly is the objection made by the other side that you are speculating, and speculation is not permitted. You are not there to speculate. You are there to talk as an expert about the logical inferences and conclusions with respect to various alternatives and their consequences.

## Practical Pointers for Direct Examination

1. The aim of testimony is to be listened to, to be believed, and to be convincing.

2. You need adequate preparation. Although even CPAs from top firms have had errors in their testimony, that doesn't mean you should have errors. You want to go through your report very carefully. The best way to find errors is to explain that report to somebody else in great detail.

3. Answer questions deliberately. Do not hurry and do not lecture.

4. Be concise; do not ramble. Good preparation will result in well-organized, crisp testimony.

5. Avoid jargon. Remember that the judge, other attorneys, and the jury (if you have a jury) may not know what you mean when

talking about financial terminology, concepts, and so on. While these things are just common sense to us, try to say things in ways that everybody can understand.

**6.** Do not nod or gesture in lieu of an answer. The court reporter can only write down words that have been spoken.

**7.** Know the weak spots in your report and discuss them with your attorney. It may be better to deal with them under direct examination than to wait for the cross-examiner to hammer on them.

## CROSS-EXAMINATION

In cross-examination, you are asked closed-end questions by the other attorney that can only be answered "yes," "no," "I don't know," and so on.

Here, Barbara Stark explains cross-examination more fully.

### Barbara:

When the direct examination is over, the other lawyer gets up to cross-examine you. With a good cross-examiner, you are the one who becomes less visible because the cross-examiner is using what we call leading questions. The cross-examiner is now telling the story and you are merely saying yes or no.

Given the breakfast topic example from the previous section on direct examination, here's how the cross-examination might sound.

*Attorney:* Your name is Carol Ann Wilson, is it not?

*You:* Yes.

*A:* Are you staying at the Sheraton Hotel?

*Y:* Yes.

*A:* The Sheraton Hotel is just across the street from The John Wayne Airport, isn't it?

*Y:* Yes, it is.

*A:* Now, Ms. Wilson, when you got up this morning, you went down to the cafe?

*Y:* Yes.

*A:* That cafe is on the first floor of the hotel?

*Y:* Yes.

*A:* And you sat down and you had breakfast?

*Y:* Yes.

*A:* When you had that breakfast, you ordered eggs, didn't you?

*Y:* Yes.

*A:* As a matter of fact, you had sausage with those eggs?

*Y:* Yes, I did.

*A:* And then you walked out of the restaurant without paying, DIDN'T you?

Do you see the difference? Cross-examinations are uncomfortable because you sense a loss of control. It is like you are being pulled here and there, and you don't know where you will end up. If it is done right, a cross-examination puts words in the witness's mouth.

*       *       *       *

There are many different approaches to cross-examination. The cross-examiner will try to attack the expert in various ways. Here are some things to watch for:

- Attacking the expert's qualifications.
- Attacking the expert's objectivity.
- Attacking the expert's methodology.
- Attacking the expert's assumptions.
- Trying to establish that the expert has bias toward the client who hired him or her.

Helen Stone adds this opinion.

### Helen:

Cross-examination is when the lawyer essentially gets to testify. The lawyer takes control and tries to put words in your mouth. The most common kind of questions that the lawyer uses are those that require only a yes or no answer. If you try to add more explanation, the lawyer is going to cut you off. The lawyer wants to show the judge that there is a different slant on this topic other then the one that you have given in your direct testimony. So, on cross-examination you will probably not be asked any questions that start with "why." Only a less-experienced or sloppy lawyer will ask you "why" and will usually get tripped up on it. The cross-examining lawyer wants to show the limits of what you have done, show whatever deficiencies there are, and show any mistakes.

## Practical Pointers for Cross-Examination

**1.** Keep your responses brief and do not volunteer information. Remember that on direct examination, you can explain fully anything that you want. On cross-examination, however, limit your answer to the narrow question asked. Then *stop talking*. Never volunteer information or answers.

**2.** Listen to your lawyer's objections. They are usually meant to alert you to a problem area.

**3.** Don't answer too quickly or you risk answering while your attorney is preparing to object. Take a breath before each answer.

**4.** Appear briskly self-confident. If the cross-examiner asks, "Did you consider that the husband might be disabled at work?" answer, "No, I did not." You cannot take into account everything.

**5.** Bring only essential documents to the witness stand.

**6.** Do not render opinions on matters of law. Even if, on the stand, the cross-examiner asks you about a legal issue, do not attempt to answer if you are not an attorney. You cannot render opinions on matters of law.

**7.** Understand the question. If you do not understand the question, ask to have it repeated. Don't be afraid to ask for clarification of unclear questions. Do not guess if you don't know the answer.

**8.** Do not be pushed to answer yes or no. Many times, they will ask you a question that you know is not a yes or no question. You might answer, "May I explain?" If they do not let you explain, that is a signal to your client's attorney to come back and ask you on the redirect to explain further. You could say, "That cannot be answered yes or no."

**9.** Avoid such phrases as "I think," "I guess," "I believe," and "I assume."

**10.** Remain silent if attorneys object during the examination.

**11.** Avoid mannerisms that signal nervousness.

**12.** Do not get overconfident.

**13.** Do not drop your voice or head, which makes people think you really do not know what you are talking about. Even if they point out a mistake, stay confident.

**14.** Tell the truth.

Barbara Stark offers these additional tips for controlling cross-examination.

## Barbara:

**1.** Listen for open-ended questions and if you get one, answer it completely. You usually won't get many such opportunities during a cross-examination, so take advantage of them.

**2.** Never forget that after the other lawyers are finished with you, your lawyer gets up and does "redirect." You know that cross-examination is putting words in your mouth and you are just dying to explain why you said yes to a cross-examination question. If you try to explain it during cross, that is considered "nonresponsive" and it will make the judge and everyone else angry. So just say yes or no and remember that your lawyer will later get up and say, "Now, you said on cross-examination that you used a 4 percent inflation rate. Can you explain to us why you did that?" This is your chance to give all the explanation that you want.

**3.** Do not, under any circumstances, get angry. This case is not about you. If you get angry, the other side wins. When you are angry, you do not look good to the judge. This increases the chance that the judge is not going to like you. Second, when you are angry, you are not listening to the question because you are thinking about yourself and how much you hate the cross-examiner. If you take it personally and get angry, you are in trouble.

**4.** Answer tough questions head-on. If it is a tough question, think about it and answer it directly. Don't forget your calculator in court.

**5.** No matter what you do, remember that the truth is never a problem. You may hate to admit to something on cross-exam because it is not good for your client, but your job is to tell the truth on the witness stand.

**6.** Remember that in some ways court is a game. Attorneys may be at each other's throat, but at the end of the day they may go to dinner together. They may be friendly, but in court they are doing their job for their clients. It is a game so do not take it personally.

## FINAL WORDS FOR THE EXPERT WITNESS

Helen Stone gives these additional tips to the expert witness.

## Helen:

One thing is common to both juries and judges. They are going to pay more attention to your testimony if it is interesting. Many witnesses are boring either because they speak in a monotone or because they present information in an ineffective way. For example, they may have a chart and merely read all its figures to the jury without adding any other detail. It's deadly boring.

Contrast this with witnesses who can really tell a story. They are linear, they present the information in a logical fashion, and they are interesting. Keep this in mind when you are making your presentation on direct examination—the more interested the judge is, the more the judge is going to pay attention to you and follow what you have to say. That becomes important as your testimony proceeds, because as soon as the judge is hooked into your testimony, the judge is going to be focusing on you and really trying to understand. That, of course, is your goal as an expert witness.

You may have to explain to the judge what you do as a Certified Financial Planner and why you are before the court. Take as much time as possible to explain yourself and, more importantly, take as much time and go into as much detail as you can explaining the method you used to establish your assumptions and scenarios. That really is the key to your testimony.

One thing to add to your methodology is a theory, or a theme, of the case. If you want to say, for example, that a 50/50 property division is really the perfect solution and explain why, then keep that in mind from the very beginning. Although it is probably not necessary to state it in your direct examination at the outset, at some point you are going to want to have that as your conclusion. It gives you a focus—it is sort of your road map.

## CHAPTER 15

# Forms and Information Needed

## CHECKLIST OF INFORMATION TO GATHER FOR THE ATTORNEY

__Name, address, and phone number of client

__Business address and phone number

__Name, address, and phone number of other party

__Name and address of lawyer representing other party

__Date of birth of each party

__Date and place of marriage

__Names and birthdates of children

__Prior marriages of each party and details of termination

__Children of prior marriages and custodial arrangements

__Length of time lived in this state

__Existence of prenuptial agreement

__Grounds for divorce

__Objectives of each party

__Date of separation

__Current employment and place of employment

__Income of each party

__Social Security number of each party

__Education/degrees/training of each party

__Job history and income potential of each party

__Employee benefits of each party

__Details of pension and profit-sharing plans of each party

__Joint assets of the parties, including

   __Real estate

   __Stocks, bonds, and other securities

   __Bank and savings accounts

   __IRAs

__Liabilities or debt of each party

__Life insurance of each party

__Separate or personal assets of each party

__Incident of domestic abuse or threats

__Financial records including

   __Bank statements

   __Tax returns

   __Applications for loans

   __Investment statements

__Family business records including

   __Type of business

   __Shareholders

   __Percentage of ownership of business

   __Bank statements of business

   __Tax returns of business

   __Applications for loans

   __Income and balance sheets

   __Financial reports

__Furniture

__Patents, royalties, and copyrights

__Collections, artwork, and antiques

__Trust funds, annuities, and inheritances

__Career assets (allowed in some states). Includes education, licenses or degrees, benefit packages, stock options, deferred compensation, vacation, sick leave, and bonuses.

## FINAL DIVORCE DECREE

After the divorce is final it is too late to find out that additional items should have been negotiated and covered in the final settlement. To make sure that the final divorce decree gives the protection wanted, use this checklist to include those items that pertain to your client's case.

**1.** The divorce process
- Who pays the legal fees?
- If the exwife must take the exhusband to court for nonsupport or for not complying with the divorce decree, will the husband pay the legal fees and court costs? Will there be interest charges?
- Does the wife want to take back her maiden name?

**2.** Property
- Who gets which property?
- Who gets which debt?
- If the pension is to be divided, has the proper paperwork been prepared?
- If there is a property settlement note, is it collateralized? Is there interest on it?
- Does the spouse who gets the house get the whole basis in the house?
- If the spouse who gets the house needs to sell it immediately, will that person be responsible for the entire capital gains tax?

**3.** Maintenance
- How much maintenance for how long?
- If maintenance is not awarded now, can it be awarded later?
- Will there be life insurance to cover maintenance in the event of the payor's death?

**4.** Child Support
- How much child support for how long?
- Will the child support change during college or when visitation times change?
- Who has custody of the children?
- What is the visitation schedule?

- Who pays related expenses for school (transportation, books, etc.) and unusual expenses (lessons, camp, teeth, etc.)?
- Who will deduct the children on income tax forms?

## FORMS

## Basic Information

The Basic Information form is for data gathering. Many times, some of these pieces of information are overlooked when meeting with the client for the first time. This form will help you to be more thorough.

You saw examples of errors in the financial affidavit in Chapter 7. The following format will help gather all pieces of information that go into putting the numbers of your case together.

# BASIC INFORMATION

1. Wife's name _____

    Address _____

    _____

    Age _____

    Phone (____) _____ day   (____) _____ evening

    Wife's attorney _____

    Phone _____

    Occupation & no. of years _____

2. Husband's name _____

    Address _____

    _____

    Age _____

    Phone (____) _____ day   (____) _____ evening

    Husband's attorney _____

    Phone _____

    Occupation & no. of years _____

3. Length of marriage—years _____

4. Number of children _____

    Name                                  Birthdate

    _____

    _____

    _____

    _____

5. Will wife work after divorce? _____

    Projected gross income _____

    Projected net income _____

6. Husband's projected gross income _____

    Husband's projected net income _____

7. Husband's settlement proposal (attach additional pages as necessary)

    Asset division _____

    Monthly maintenance _____

    How long maintenance will continue _____

    Monthly child support (per child) _____

    How long child support will continue _____

    Contribution to children's college expenses _____

8. Wife's settlement proposal (attach additional pages as necessary)

    Asset division _____

    Monthly maintenance _____

How long maintenance will continue _____
Monthly child support (per child) _____
How long child support will continue _____
Contribution to children's college expenses _____

9. Residence

Fair market value of home _____
Remaining balance of the mortgage _____
Years remaining to pay _____
Interest rate _____
Monthly payment (PITI) _____
Basis in the house _____
Will the house be sold? _____
If not, who wants to stay in the house? _____

10. Please provide the following information:

List of assets (Provide information on each that applies.)
    Checking and savings accounts
    CDs
    Annuities
    Stocks and bonds
    Mutual funds
    Real estate (rentals, second home, land, etc.)
    Limited partnerships
    Life insurance policies
    Family business
      Percent of ownership
      Tax returns
      Financial statements
    IRAs
    401(k) or other retirement plans
    Defined-benefit pension plan (future payments at retirement)
    Debt (credit card, loans, etc.)
    Vehicles
    Personal possessions
    Antiques and collectibles
    Personal or separate property
Last three years' tax returns
Paycheck stubs
Financial affidavit for husband and wife (shows income and expenses)
Information on pension and retirement plans

**ALL INFORMATION IS STRICTLY CONFIDENTIAL**

# FINANCIAL AFFIDAVIT

Name _____

1. Job title or occupation _____

2. Primary employer's name _____
   Hours worked per week _____

3. I am paid ☐weekly ☐every other week ☐twice each month ☐monthly
   Amount of each check (gross) _____

4. Monthly gross income _____

5. Monthly payroll deductions
   (Number of exemptions being claimed: _____)
   Federal income tax _____
   Social Security _____
   Medicare _____
   State income tax _____
   Health insurance premium _____
   Life insurance premium _____
   Dental insurance premium _____
   401(k) _____
        Total deductions from this employment _____

6. Net monthly take-home pay from primary employer _____

7. Other sources and amounts of income
   SOURCE                AMOUNT
   _____        _____

   _____        _____

8. Deductions from other income sources listed in Part 7
   DEDUCTIONS            AMOUNT
   _____        _____

   _____        _____

9. Net monthly income from other sources _____

10. NET MONTHLY INCOME from ALL sources _____

11. Net monthly income of children _____

12. Income reported on last federal return _____

13. Monthly gross income of other party _____
    Monthly net income of other party _____

14. MONTHLY EXPENSES for _____ adult and _____ children:

    A. HOUSING
       Rent _____
       First mortgage _____
       Second mortgage _____
       Homeowner's fee _____
                                    TOTAL HOUSING _____

    B. UTILITIES
       Gas and electric _____
       Telephone _____
       Water and sewer _____
       Trash collection _____
       Cable TV _____
                                    TOTAL UTILITIES _____

    C. FOOD
       Grocery store items _____
       Restaurant meals _____
                                    TOTAL FOOD _____

    D. MEDICAL (after insurance)
       Doctor _____
       Dentist _____
       Prescriptions _____
       Therapy _____
                                    TOTAL MEDICAL _____

    E. INSURANCE
       Life insurance _____
       Health insurance _____
       Dental insurance _____
       Homeowner's insurance _____
                                    TOTAL INSURANCE _____

F. TRANSPORTATION
 Vehicle 1 _____
  Payment _____
  Fuel _____
  Repair and maintenance _____
  Insurance _____
  Parking _____
 Vehicle 2_____
  Payment _____
  Fuel _____
  Repair and maintenance _____
  Insurance _____
  Parking _____
        TOTAL TRANSPORTATION _____

G. CLOTHING    TOTAL CLOTHING _____

H. LAUNDRY    TOTAL LAUNDRY _____

I. CHILD CARE (and related)
 Child care _____
 Allowance_____
        TOTAL CHILD CARE _____

J. EDUCATION (and related)
 For children
  School costs _____
  Lunches
  Sports _____
 For spouse
  Tuition _____
  Books and fees _____
        TOTAL EDUCATION _____

K. RECREATION
 Entertainment _____
 Hobbies _____
 Vacations _____
 Memberships/clubs _____
        TOTAL RECREATION _____

L. MISCELLANEOUS
Gifts _____
Hair care/nail care _____
Pet care _____
Books/newspapers _____
Donations _____

TOTAL MISCELLANEOUS _____

M. TOTAL REQUIRED MONTHLY EXPENSES _____

15. DEBTS

| Creditor | Unpaid Balance | Monthly Payment |
|---|---|---|
| A. _____ | $_____ | $_____ |
| B. _____ | $_____ | $_____ |
| C. _____ | $_____ | $_____ |
| D. _____ | $_____ | $_____ |
| E. _____ | $_____ | $_____ |

16. ASSETS

A. Real estate
Location _____
Market value_____
Loan _____
Net equity _____

Location _____
Market value_____
Loan _____
Net equity _____

TOTAL REAL ESTATE (NET) _____

B. FURNITURE
Location _____
Market value _____

Location _____
Market value _____

TOTAL FURNITURE_____

## C. MOTOR VEHICLES

Year/make  _____

Market value  _____

Loan _____

Net equity  _____

Year/make  _____

Market value  _____

Loan _____

Net equity  _____

TOTAL VEHICLES  _____

## D. BANK ACCOUNTS

Name of bank  _____

Current balance  _____

Name of bank  _____

Current balance  _____

Name of bank  _____

Current balance  _____

TOTAL BANKS  _____

## E. STOCKS AND BONDS

Stock name  _____

No. of shares  _____

Market value  _____

Stock name  _____

No. of shares  _____

Market value  _____

TOTAL STOCKS/BONDS  _____

## F. LIFE INSURANCE

Company name  _____

Policy number  _____

Owner's name  _____

Insured's name _____

Beneficiary's name  _____

Face value  _____

Cash surrender value  _____

Company name _____
Policy number _____
Owner's name _____
Insured's name _____
Beneficiary's name _____
Face value _____
Cash surrender value _____

Company name _____
Policy number _____
Owner's name _____
Insured's name _____
Beneficiary's name _____
Face value _____
Cash surrender value _____

TOTAL INSURANCE _____

## G. PENSION, PROFIT SHARING, RETIREMENT FUNDS

Plan name _____
Participant name _____
Value _____

Plan name _____
Participant name _____
Value _____

TOTAL PENSION _____

TOTAL ASSETS _____

## CHAPTER 16

# The Final Word

At the start of this book, my objective was to illustrate that divorce could be fair to both parties. Yet it is also obvious that divorce is rarely easy. Perhaps people should look at what it takes to get divorced before they get married. With all the time and money and emotion involved, it might make potential spouses think hard about whether they are getting married for the right reason. If they're not, it would allow them to reconsider getting married in the first place.

However, even this knowledge won't stop many from getting married—and then, unfortunately, divorced. There is a type of insanity that seems to surface when a divorce is imminent. Otherwise, why would rational people divorce? Men and women say and do horrible things to each other—things that they would never have imagined they would say and do to someone they loved and cared for at one time.

Someone once said that the cost of divorce averages $20,000 per couple. If this is true, Americans are needlessly spending $28 billion on divorce *every year!* And the work-force suffers because it's not easy to leave the emotions outside the door of the office. Added to that are the anger, bitterness, and vindictiveness that tear families apart.

Well-informed financial advisors like you can do a lot toward helping people achieve equitable settlements and minimize the negative, destructive forces of divorce. In fact, the wave of the future is having teams of experts who can help people through the difficult times of breaking up a family. This team can help the divorcing couple stay out of court.

Who makes up this team?

1. The attorney is critical to the team. Legal documents need to be drawn up. New wills may need to be made. Pensions need to be divided via a legal document.

2. The financial expert—whether it be a Certified Public Accountant (CPA), Certified Divorce Planner (CDP), Certified Financial Planner (CFP), or other financial planner—can help the attorney look at basis in property, how assets will be taxed, how pensions are valued, the long-term effect of dividing property and maintenance, and how inflation assumptions will affect these decisions.

3. Real estate appraisers, business appraisers, and other asset appraisers are needed to place values on different pieces of property so that property settlement negotiations can take place.

4. Mediators can work with the couple in the beginning to get as many agreements as they can and possibly reach a settlement.

5. Therapists are needed when the emotions are so strong that the issues are clouded. Each person needs to know of her worth. Each person also needs to take responsibility for himself as much as possible.

6. Career counselors can test and evaluate a spouse who has been out of the workplace for a long time to see what the future might hold for this person and where he or she might best concentrate job skills or talents.

It is well known among judges, attorneys, and other professionals in the divorce arena that people burn out faster here than in any other legal career. Divorce judges change venue when they can't take the negative emotional atmosphere in the court anymore. Criminal court becomes more desirable than divorce court! Divorce attorneys retire early or become mediators or maybe even open a cooking school!

My vision is that all the professionals work together to minimize the negative impact of divorce. Attorneys help their clients settle out of court. Judges hand down more equitable settlements. Financial advisors provide the essential information to help in the decision making. And in the end, Americans will have more money available to keep them on the positive side of cash flow instead of being in debt, and children in divorced families will have fewer deep emotional scars. Who knows, maybe the crime rate will even decrease!

I believe the key to all this lies with you, the financial advisor. Laws change. The economic environment changes. You must have the tenacity and experience to flow with these changes.

Simple? No, but when is anything worthwhile simple? Do what makes common sense. Have patience. Keep learning. I believe in your ability to put it together. Now it's your turn.

## CHAPTER 17

# Resources

## BOOKS ON DIVORCE

*After Marriage Ends: Economic Consequences for Midlife Women.* Leslie A. Morgan. Newbury Park, CA. Sage Publications. 1991.

*Between Love and Hate: A Guide to Civilized Divorce.* Lois Gold. New York. Plume. 1992.

*The Boys and Girls Book about Divorce.* Richard Gardner. New York. Science House.

*The Complete Guide for Men and Women Divorcing.* Melvin Belli and Mel Krantzler. New York. St. Martin's Press. 1990.

*The Consequences of Divorce: Economic and Custodial Impact on Children and Adults.* Craig A. Everett. Binghamton, NY. Haworth Press. 1991.

*Creative Divorce: A New Opportunity for Personal Growth.* Mel Krantzler. New York. Signet. 1974.

*Divorce and Money: Everything You Need to Know about Dividing Property.* Violet Woodhouse and Victoria Felton-Collins. Berkeley, CA. Nolo Press.

*Divorce and New Beginnings: An Authoritative Guide to Recovery and Growth, Solo Parenting, and Step Families.* Genevieve Clapp. New York. John Wiley & Sons. 1992.

*Divorce and Taxes.* Chicago. Commerce Clearing House. 1992.

*Divorce: A Woman's Guide to Getting a Fair Share.* Patricia Phillips and George Mair. New York. Macmillan. 1995.

*Divorce Decisions Workbook: A Planning and Action Guide.* Margorie L. Engel and Diana D. Gould. New York. McGraw Hill. 1992.

*The Divorce Handbook: Your Basic Guide to Divorce.* James T. Friedman. New York. Random House. 1984.

*Divorce Help Sourcebook.* Margorie L. Engel. Detroit. Visible Ink Press. 1994.

*The Divorce Revolution: The Unexpected Social and Economic Consequences for Women and Children in America.* Lenore Weitzman. New York. The Free Press (a Division of Macmillan, Inc.). 1985.

*Divorcing.* Mel Krantzler and Melvin M. Belli, Sr. New York. St. Martin's Press. 1988.

*The Dollars and Sense of Divorce: The Financial Guide for Women.* Judith Briles. New York: Ballantine. 1991.

*The Expert Witness Handbook: Tips and Techniques for the Litigation Consultant.* Dan Poynter. Santa Barbara, CA. ParaP. 1987.

*Fair Share Divorce for Women.* Kathleen Miller. Bellevue, WA. Miller, Bird Advisors. 1995.

*Financial Fitness through Divorce: A Guide to the Financial Realities of Divorce.* Elizabeth S. Lewin. New York. Facts on File Publications. 1987.

*The Financial Guide to Divorce: Everything You Need to Know for Financial Strategies during and after Divorce.* Frances Johansen. Irvine, CA. United Resources Press. 1991.

*Financial Planning from We to Me: Divorce Strategies to Help You Get More of What You Want.* Kathleen L. Cotton. Lynwood, WA. Wealth Books. 1996.

*The Five-Minute Lawyer's Guide to Divorce.* Michael Allan Cane. New York. Dell. 1995.

*Friendly Divorce Guidebook for Colorado.* M. Arden Hauer and S. W. "Wendy" Whicher. Denver, CO. Bradford. 1994.

*The Good Divorce: Keeping Your Family Together When Your Marriage Comes Apart.* Constance Ahrons. New York. Harper Perennial. 1994.

*A Guide to Divorce Mediation: How to Reach a Fair, Legal Settlement at a Fraction of the Cost.* Gary J. Friedman. New York. Workman Publishing. 1993.

*Handbook of Financial Planning for Divorce and Separation: 1993 Cumulative Supplement.* D. Larry Crumbley. New York. John Wiley & Sons. 1993.

*In Defense of Children: Understanding the Rights, Needs and Interests of the Child.* Thomas A. Nazario. New York. Charles Scribner's Sons, Bennett Publishing Co. 1988.

*Money Sense: What Every Woman Must Know to Be Financially Confident.* Judith Briles. Chicago. Moody. 1995.

*Rebuilding: When Your Relationship Ends.* Dr. Bruce Fisher. San Luis Obispo, CA. Impact. 1995.

*Smart Ways to Save Money during and after Divorce.* Victoria Felton-Collins and Ginita Wall. Berkeley, CA. Nolo Press. 1994.

*Succeeding as an Expert Witness: Increasing Your Impact and Income.* Harold A. Feder. Glenwood Springs, CO. Tageh Press. 1993.

*Survival Manual for Men in Divorce.* Edwin Schilling III and Carol Ann Wilson. Dubuque, IA. Kendall Hunt Publishing. 1994.

*Survival Manual for Women in Divorce.* Carol Ann Wilson and Edwin Schilling III. Dubuque, IA. Kendall Hunt Publishing. 1994.

*Tax Strategies in Divorce: 1992 Supplement.* Dennis C. Mahoney. New York. John Wiley & Sons. 1992.

*A Woman's Guide to Divorce and Decision Making.* Christina Robertson. New York. Simon & Schuster. 1989.

*You're Entitled: A Divorce Lawyer Talks to Women.* Sidney M. DeAngelis. Chicago. Contemporary Books. 1989.

## DIVORCE SOFTWARE

**AEQUUS**
Aequus Financial Services
303 W. Erie, Suite 311
Chicago, IL 60610
312–664–4090
$795

Spreadsheets, cash flow
analysis, asset summaries

**DIVORCE PLAN**™
Quantum Financial, Inc.
2724 Winding Trail Place
Boulder, CO 80304
800–875–1760
$400

Spreadsheets, graphs, net worth
comparisons

**FinPlan's DIVORCE**
  **PLANNER®**
FinPlan Co.
100 E. Cuttriss Street
Park Ridge, IL 60068
800–777–2108
$400

Tax and support
planning for divorce


## LEGAL AND MEDIATION ASSOCIATIONS

**American Academy of Family**
  **Mediators**
4 Militia Drive
Lexington, MA 02173
617–674–2663

**American Bar Association**
750 N. Lake Shore Drive
Chicago, IL 60611
312–988–5000
800–621–6159

**American Academy of Matrimonial**
  **Lawyers**
150 N. Michigan Ave., Suite 2040
Chicago, IL 60601
312–263–6477

# STATE RESOURCES

*Alabama*
**Alabama State Bar**
415 Dexter Street
PO Box 671
Montgomery, AL 36104
205–269–1515

*Alaska*
**Alaska Bar Association**
510 L Street, No. 602
PO Box 100279
Anchorage, AK 99510
907–272–7469

*Arizona*
**American Arbitration Association**
Phoenix Regional Office
333 E. Osborn Road, Suite 310
Phoenix, AZ 85012
602–234–0950
**State Bar of Arizona**
363 N. 1st Avenue
Phoenix, AZ 85003
602–252–4804

*Arkansas*
**Arkansas Bar Association**
400 W. Markham
Little Rock, AR 72201
501–375–4605

*California*
**American Arbitration Association**
Los Angeles Regional Office
443 Shatto Place
PO Box 57994
Los Angeles, CA 90020
213–383–6516

**American Arbitration Association**
Orange County, CA Regional Office
2601 Main Street, Suite 240
Irvine, CA 92714
714–474–5090

**American Arbitration Association**
San Diego Regional Office
525 C Street, Suite 400
San Diego, CA 92101
619–239–3051

**American Arbitration Association**
San Francisco Regional Office
417 Montgomery Street, 5th Floor
San Francisco, CA 94101
415–981–3901

**State Bar of California**
555 Franklin Street
San Francisco, CA 94102
415–561–8200

*Colorado*
**American Arbitration Association**
Denver Regional Office
1660 Lincoln Street, Suite 2150
Denver, CO 80264
303–831–0823

**Colorado Bar Association**
1900 Grant Street, Suite 950
Denver, CO 80203
303–860–1115

*Connecticut*
**American Arbitration Association**
Hartford Regional Office
11 Founders Place, 17th Floor
Hartford, CT 06108
203–289–3993

**Connecticut Bar Association**
101 Corporate Place
Rocky Hill, CT 06067
203–721–0025

*Delaware*
**Delaware State Bar Association**
1225 King Street
Wilmington, DE 19801
302–658–5279

*District of Columbia*
**American Arbitration Association**
Washington, DC, Regional Office
1150 Connecticut Avenue NW, 6th
 Floor
Washington, DC 20036
202–296–8510
**Bar Association of the District of
Columbia**
1819 H Street NW, 12th Floor
Washington, DC 20006
202–223–6600
**District of Columbia Bar**
1250 H Street NW, 6th Floor
Washington, DC 20005
202–737–4700
*Florida*
**American Arbitration Association**
Miami Regional Office
99 SE 5th Street, Suite 200
Miami, FL 33131
305–358–7777
**American Arbitration Association**
Orlando Regional Office
201 E. Pine Street, Suite 800
Orlando, FL 32801
407–648–1185
**Florida Bar**
The Florida Bar Center
650 Apalachee Parkway
Tallahassee, FL 32399
904–561–5600
*Georgia*
**American Arbitration Association**
Atlanta Regional Office
1360 Peachtree Street NE, Suite 270
Atlanta, GA 30361
404–872–3022

**State Bar of Georgia**
800 The Hurt Building
50 Hurt Plaza
Atlanta, GA 30303
404–527–8700
*Hawaii*
**American Arbitration Association**
Honolulu Regional Office
810 Richards Street, Suite 641
Honolulu, HI 96813
808–531–0541
**Hawaii State Bar Association**
Penthouse, 9th Floor
1136 Union Mall
Honolulu, HI 96813
808–537–1868
*Idaho*
**Idaho State Bar**
PO Box 895
Boise, ID 83701
208–342–8958
*Illinois*
**American Arbitration Association**
Chicago Regional Office
225 N. Michigan Avenue, Suite 2527
Chicago, IL 60601
312–616–6560
**Illinois State Bar Association**
424 S. 2nd Street
Springfield, IL 62701
217–525–1760
*Indiana*
**Indiana State Bar Association**
230 E. Ohio Street, 4th Floor
Indianapolis, IN 46204
317–639–5465
*Iowa*
**Iowa State Bar Association**
521 E. Locust
Des Moines, IA 50309
515–243–3179

*Kansas*
**Kansas Bar Association**
1200 Harrison Street
Topeka, KS 66612
913–234–5696

*Kentucky*
**Kentucky Bar Association**
514 W. Main Street
Frankfort, KY 40601
502–564–3795

*Louisiana*
**American Arbitration Association**
New Orleans Regional Office
650 Poydras Street, Suite 1535
New Orleans, LA 70130
504–522–8781

**Louisiana State Bar Association**
601 St. Charles Avenue
New Orleans, LA 70130
504–566–1600

*Maine*
**Maine State Bar Association**
124 State Street
Box 788
Augusta, ME 04330
207–622–7523

*Maryland*
**Maryland State Bar Association Inc.**
520 W. Fayette Street
Baltimore, MD 21201
410–685–7878

*Massachusetts*
**American Arbitration Association**
Boston Regional Office
133 Federal Street
Boston, MA 02110
617–451–6600

**Massachusetts Bar Association**
20 West Street
Boston, MA 02111
617–542–3602

*Michigan*
**American Arbitration Association**
Southfield, MI, Regional Office
10 Oak Hollow Street, Suite 170
Southfield, MI 48034
313–352–5500

**State Bar of Michigan**
306 Townsend Street
Lansing, MI 48933
517–372–9030

*Minnesota*
**American Arbitration Association**
Minneapolis Regional Office
514 Nicollet Mall, Suite 670
Minneapolis, MN 55402
612–332–6545

**Minnesota State Bar Association**
514 Nicollet Mall, Suite 300
Minneapolis, MN 55402
612–333–1183

*Mississippi*
**Mississippi State Bar**
643 N. State Street
Jackson, MS 39202
601–948–4471

*Missouri*
**American Arbitration Association**
Kansas City Regional Office
1101 Walnut Street, Suite 903
Kansas City, MO 64106
816–221–6401

**American Arbitration Association**
St. Louis Regional Office
1 Mercantile Center, Suite 2512
St. Louis, MO 63101
314–621–7175

**Missouri Bar**
326 Monroe
Jefferson City, MO 65102
314–635–4128

*Montana*
**State Bar of Montana**
46 N. Last Chance Gulch
Box 577
Helena, MT 59624
406–442–7660

*Nebraska*
**Nebraska State Bar Association**
635 S. 14th Street, 2d Floor
Lincoln, NE 68508
402–475–7091

*Nevada*
**State Bar of Nevada**
201 Las Vegas Blvd., Suite 200
Las Vegas, NV 89101
702–382–2200

*New Hampshire*
**New Hampshire Bar Association**
112 Pleasant Street
Concord, NH 03301
603–224–6942

*New Jersey*
**American Arbitration Association**
Somerset Regional Office
265 Davidson Avenue, Suite 140
Somerset, NJ 08873
908–560–9560

**New Jersey State Bar Association**
New Jersey Law Center
1 Constitution Square
New Brunswick, NJ 08901
908–249–5000

*New Mexico*
**State Bar of New Mexico**
121 Tijeras Street, NE
Albuquerque, NM 87102
505–842–6132

*New York*
**American Arbitration Association**
Garden City, NY, Regional Office
666 Old Country Road, Suite 603
Garden City, NY 11530
516–222–1660

**American Arbitration Association**
New York Regional Office
140 W. 51st Street
New York, NY 10020
212–484–4000

**American Arbitration Association**
Syracuse Regional Office
205 S. Salina Street
Syracuse, NY 13202
315–472–5483

**American Arbitration Association**
White Plains, NY, Regional Office
34 S. Broadway
White Plains, NY 10601
914–946–1119

**New York State Bar Association**
1 Elk Street
Albany, NY 12207
518–463–3200

*North Carolina*
**American Arbitration Association**
Charlotte Regional Office
428 E. 4th Street, Suite 300
Charlotte, NC 28202
704–347–0200

**North Carolina Bar Association**
1312 Annapolis Drive
Box 12806
Raleigh, NC 27608
919–828–0561

**North Carolina State Bar**
208 Fayetteville Street Mall
Raleigh, NC 27611
919–828–4620

*North Dakota*
**State Bar Association of North Dakota**
515 ½ E. Broadway, Suite 101
Bismarck, ND 58502
701–255–1404

*Ohio*
**American Arbitration Association**
Cincinnati Regional Office
441 Vine Street, Suite 3308
Cincinnati, OH 45202
513–241–8434

**American Arbitration Association**
Middleburg Heights Regional Office
17900 Jefferson Road, Suite 101
Middleburg Heights, OH 44130
216–891–4741

**Ohio State Bar Association**
1700 Lake Shore Drive
Columbus, OH 43216
614–487–2050

*Oklahoma*
**Oklahoma Bar Association**
1901 N. Lincoln
Oklahoma City, OK 73105
405–524–2365

*Oregon*
**Oregon State Bar**
5200 SW Meadows Road
Box 1689
Lake Oswego, OR 97035
503–620–0222

*Pennsylvania*
**American Arbitration Association**
Philadelphia Regional Office
230 S. Broad Street
Philadelphia, PA 19102
215–732–5260

**American Arbitration Association**
Pittsburgh Regional Office
4 Gateway Center, Room 419
Pittsburgh, PA 15222
412–261–3617

**Pennsylvania Bar Association**
100 South Street
Box 186
Harrisburg, PA 17108
717–238–6715

*Rhode Island*
**American Arbitration Association**
Providence Regional Office
115 Cedar Street
Providence, RI 02903
401–453–3250

**Rhode Island Bar Association**
115 Cedar Street
Providence, RI 02903
401–421–5740

*South Carolina*
**South Carolina Bar**
950 Taylor Street
Box 608
Columbia, SC 29202
803–799–6653

*South Dakota*
**State Bar of South Dakota**
222 E. Capitol
Pierre, SD 57501
605–224–7554

*Tennessee*
**American Arbitration Association**
Nashville Regional Office
221 4th Avenue, N., 2d Floor
Nashville, TN 37219
615–256–5857

**Tennessee Bar Association**
3622 West End Avenue
Nashville, TN 37205
615–383–7421

*Texas*
**American Arbitration Association**
Dallas Regional Office
2 Galleria Tower, Suite 1440
Dallas, TX 75240
214–702–8222

**American Arbitration Association**
Houston Regional Office
1001 Fannin Street, Suite 1005
Houston, TX 77002
713–739–1302

**State Bar of Texas**
1414 Colorado
Box 12487
Austin, TX 78711
512–463–1400

*Utah*
**American Arbitration Association**
Salt Lake City Regional Office
645 S. 200 E., Suite 203
Salt Lake City, UT 84111
801–531–9748

**Utah State Bar**
645 S. 200 E., Suite 310
Salt Lake City, UT 84111
801–531–9077

*Vermont*
**Vermont Bar Association**
Box 100
Montpelier, VT 05601
802–223–2020

*Virginia*
**Virginia Bar Association**
701 E. Franklin Street, Suite 1515
Richmond, VA 23219
804–644–0041

**Virginia State Bar**
707 E. Main Street, Suite 1500
Richmond, VA 23219
804–775–0500

*Washington*
**American Arbitration Association**
Seattle Regional Office
1325 4th Avenue, Suite 1414
Seattle, WA 98101
206–622–6435

**Washington State Bar Association**
500 Westin Building
2001 6th Avenue
Seattle, WA 98121
206–727–8200

*West Virginia*
**West Virginia Bar Association**
904 Security Building
100 Capitol Street
Charleston, WV 25301
304–342–1474

**West Virginia State Bar**
2006 Kanawha Blvd., E.
Charleston, WV 25311
304–558–2456

*Wisconsin*
**State Bar of Wisconsin**
402 W. Wilson Street
Madison, WI 53703
608–257–3838

*Wyoming*
**Wyoming State Bar**
500 Randall Avenue
Cheyenne, WY 82001
307–632–9061

# INDEX